# TORCHES TOGETHER

The Rhön Bruderhof

The Alm Bruderhof

# TORCHES TOGETHER

## The Beginning and Early Years
## of the Bruderhof Communities

by

# Emmy Arnold

PLOUGH PUBLISHING HOUSE

 Rifton, New York

Translated from the German
by the Society of Brothers
(Bruderhof)
at Rifton, New York


First edition     1964
Second edition    1971

ISBN 87486-109-8
Library of Congress Catalog Card Number:
77-166341
Printed at the Plough Press, Farmington, Pa., U.S.A.

# CONTENTS

Wherefore burn poor and lonely
    As one needy brand?
Torches together, hand to hand!

He who feels deep within him
A fire burning bright
Must through that glow
With his brothers unite.

Wherefore burn poor and lonely
As one needy brand?
Torches together, hand to hand!

*Otto Salomon*

Whitsun Conference, 1920 (p. 33)

Sannerz (p. 36)

# SEEKING

AS I WAS ASKED to write down the story of our life,[1] and
as I am the only one left who experienced the early beginnings, I want to try to write down a little of all I remember
especially well. Others may continue, those who also experienced much of that which moved us during the early years of
our communal history—how we were visited again and again
and kindled by the uniting Spirit, in spite of our human weaknesses and failings. On his fiftieth birthday Eberhard, conscious
of our shortcomings, said to the brotherhood and to the household circle assembled on July 26, 1933, "It is a miracle that
we can still be a part of this."

I don't really know where to begin, for the history of our
previous lives somehow belongs to it all. However, I will only
touch on it quite briefly. We both stem from academic circles.
Both of us enjoyed a very protected childhood; yes, we were
rather isolated from other kinds of people. Although we, and
this is true of both of us, owe a great debt of gratitude to our
parents, yet in a way we always went our own ways. Somehow
we did not feel that our lives were complete. We were longing
for a fuller life. We could not help feeling a certain boredom.

[1] The Bruderhof or Society of Brothers.

Eberhard Arnold was born on July 26, 1883 in Königsberg, East Prussia. His father, Carl Franklin Arnold, born in Williamsfield, Ohio, in the United States on March 10, 1853, taught in the grammar school in Königsberg at the time Eberhard was born. Eberhard's mother Elisabeth, née Voigt, came from traditional academic circles. She was born on September 20, 1852 in Oldenburg. Eberhard was the third child in the family. He had one brother and three sisters. When he was still a young boy his father accepted the chair of Theology and Church History at the University of Breslau in Silesia.

They told me that in his boyhood days Eberhard was a very lively boy, full of mischief, and that he caused quite a lot of trouble, especially for his teachers. They as well as the parents of his schoolmates were not always too pleased with the kind of influence he had on them. Already at that time he stood in opposition to his parents, because he felt drawn to poor people and tramps. He found these people much more natural and warmhearted than those of the middle class. This kind of thing was hard for his family to understand, and a number of conflicts were the result; for instance, when Eberhard traded his new hat for that of a tramp, and his mother discovered lice soon afterwards.

At the age of sixteen Eberhard could not feel satisfied any longer with the kind of life he was living. He spent his summer vacation at the rectory of his uncle, Ernst Ferdinand Klein, at Lichtenrade near Berlin. Here he came into contact with a kind of Christianity he had never known before. E. F. Klein, through his experience of Christ, took his stand completely with the poor — at that time with the badly underpaid weavers. This brought him a good deal of hostility from his parishioners. People threw stones at his windows, and it was not at all clear whether he would be able to continue in his parish.

Once Eberhard was present during a talk his uncle had with a young officer of the Salvation Army. He followed what was said with eager interest. The brotherly way in which these two men conversed with each other and the love to Christ which he found present in both aroused in the sixteen-year-old boy a deep longing to find the source of this himself. After his return from this vacation he began to seek it. It was a moving time of much inner seeking to find Christ. Eberhard told me how he visited a young pastor one day, after hearing him speak. When he asked him about the Holy Spirit he answered, "It is just this Spirit who has led you here to me." It then happened that Eberhard, after a prolonged inner struggle, experienced Christ in October of 1899, when he was still a young lad of sixteen.

Eberhard was very moved when he told me about this time in his life. It was the same period when the so-called Fellowship Movement became very widespread. It arose in England and America, but also grew in Germany, Sweden, Switzerland, and other countries. Those who were in this movement experienced Christ as their Redeemer. Many people from all sectors of the population found liberation from their sins in the numerous revival meetings of that period, including those of the Salvation Army. But there was more than that. People came together in private homes, forming groups and fellowships in which they witnessed and worshiped together. Something had really begun to move. Immediately after his own conversion Eberhard tried to get in close contact with these groups.

As a first step he talked with his parents and teachers in an effort to put things right. Alas, they neither understood nor believed him. One teacher even believed that Eberhard was playing a joke on them and sent him out of the room as a prankster! But step by step people began to accept the fact that he was in bitter earnest, most of all his schoolmates. They soon gathered around him and a small movement came into being among them. As a result, Eberhard's room was hardly ever empty. He had great difficulty in applying himself to his studies and continuing at school.

The situation became worse when Eberhard began to associate with Salvation Army folks as a fruit of his search for people who were trying to put Christianity into action and who showed a real love for their fellowmen. He attended their meetings frequently, and together with them he visited some of the darkest taverns of Breslau and its environs at nighttime. He was trying to save those who were lost and to reach out to the most desperate and downtrodden people of the "submerged tenth," as old Salvation Army General William Booth used to call these unfortunates.

This development caused a great deal of excitement at home. His parents read large billposters all over the town saying, "Attention! Salvation Army. Tonight missionary Eberhard Arnold will speak in a big meeting." Actually grammar school boys were forbidden by law to engage in any kind of public speaking. This kind of thing made the existing conflict between Eberhard and his parents even worse. His father was convinced already then, as he was later on several occasions, that he would be forced to give up his university chair because his ill-mannered son was destroying his good name.

When an opportunity arose, Eberhard's parents made use of it and sent him to the little town of Jauer for further studies. Before that the school authorities had put an end to his public appearances. There at Jauer, Eberhard was to prepare for his final exams undisturbed by all these interruptions. Even there a small group of students gathered around him to meet for regular Bible study. However, Eberhard was able to graduate in spite of this. Many years later, also since Eberhard's death, we still met people in various places who were never able to forget this time of first love and searching, people who received a direction for their whole lives during this period.

At first Eberhard was wondering whether he should not join the Salvation Army. During one summer when vacationing at the North Sea, he fought this question through. It was his love for those who are lost, who are unjustly treated and to whom Christ has come in a special way, which bound him very closely to these people who were making such great sacrifices. Yet he realized more and more that they approached things in a rather one-sided way and that they lacked a certain depth in their facing of the various problems with which life confronts us.

He decided, then, not to join the Salvation Army. But he continued at all times to feel a special sense of friendship and love for these people. Right to the end of his life he continued to visit their meetings and even to speak there, if a word was given to him, thus continuing with the friendship he felt for them. I could tell a good deal more from what Eberhard himself told me about this time, or from what I heard from his brother and his sisters, but most of all from his mother, who had a special love for him. Her stories were often full of humor, but often also full of seriousness.

Now I will try to tell a few things about my own childhood and youth. I was born on December 25, 1884 in Riga, Latvia, as the second child of my father, Heinrich von Hollander, and my mother Monika, née Otto. There were five girls and two boys in our family. I remember little of my early childhood in my native town of Riga, because I was only five years old when we left our homeland. Riga had come more and more under Russian influence, and we, like many other German-Baltic families, emigrated to Germany to withdraw from this influence. I never saw Riga again. It was in the spring of 1890 that we left to settle in Jena at first. They tell me that I was quite a wild little girl; there was no tree too high for me to climb and no train rushed by fast enough but that I tried to keep up with it by running.

When I entered school in the spring of 1891 I had little interest in learning and my teachers did not find it too easy. I could hardly wait for recess or the end of school to get to my play and to other new pranks. But in spite of all this wildness and naughtiness something different, an urge toward God, made itself felt in me. When my little brother died suddenly at the age of nine months, I pondered a good deal about the question as to where he and others who had died would be, and when I looked up to the stars I wondered whether he might be on one of them.

Later, after we had moved to Halle, I was among the troublemakers at first. Though I was only thirteen then, I experienced, in connection with my friend Lisa Franke, an urge toward God and Christ; but I never spoke about this. In my family we were extremely reserved in the use of religious terms. However, it was noticed that I began to go to church and to attend religious meetings on my own, and that I got hold of books such as those by Zinzendorf and about him, or Otto Franke's *Footprints of the Living God on My Way of Life*, or Thomas a Kempis' *Imitation of Christ*.

When our youngest sister Margarethe died a little later as a result of appendicitis—she was fourteen years old then—I made the decision, after much deliberation, to give a meaning to my life rather than to spend it, empty and meaningless, just as a daughter in the family together with my sisters. Again, this decision came about through my friend Lisa Franke. It was my wish to become a deaconess to help the sick, especially sick children. Thus I entered the Deaconess

Home in Halle in the spring of 1902 as a helper. I was then seventeen years old. In the beginning I helped out for only a few days every week relieving other nurses, but soon I got a full-time job in the children's home or ward where I learned to know much suffering in children.

In 1905, as a girl of twenty, I became a probationer nurse, as I had now reached the proper age. At first I worked in the women's wards. The day was long and the work hard. There was no "eight-hour day." All this gave me a great sense of joy. However, I returned home after a few months, partly for reasons of health. Later I entered the district hospital at Salzwedel, where I nursed men for a whole year. Two of the young men whom I nursed died as a result of typhus, in an epidemic. This again challenged me to dedicate fully the days or weeks given to me to something of significance beyond this life.

I went home for my vacation. What was to happen to me at home, what I was to experience there, was completely new to me and very exciting and moving. Actually I had only intended to stay at home for a few weeks of rest, as I felt an inner vocation for the task I had chosen to do.

At that time Ludwig von Gerdtell had just completed a series of lectures in the largest hall of Halle. His topics had been "The Atonement of Christ," "Can modern man still believe in the Resurrection of Jesus?" "Is there sufficient historical evidence that Christ rose from the dead?" and others. I was drawn into the experience and came under the spell of these lectures more and more through the accounts of my brother and sisters, but also through other friends and acquaintances, even through business contacts, although I myself had not heard von Gerdtell.

As the saying then went, "All of Halle is standing on its head." People would address complete strangers in the street and ask them what they thought of these lectures. I managed to get hold of them in print, and all of a sudden I was a part of this movement, its call to repentance and to a radical change of life. With sharp words the call had rung out: "Repent! for the Kingdom of Heaven is at hand." I felt personally hit and sought contact with the people who were part of this movement. I began to clear up my own life and to put myself under the judgment of the message.

People from all kinds of circles, in Halle mainly those who belonged to academic or the so-called better circles, joined this movement. They would meet in private homes, as for instance in the house of Mrs. Else Baer, wife of the Surgeon General, or of Mrs. Schulze, wife of a leading ophthalmologist. These women opened their large drawing rooms for meetings, lectures and discussions. People like Paul Zander (who was to become a famous surgeon) and his fiancée Lene Örtling, Karl Heim, and Sigmund von Salwürk (a very well-known artist and painter) had turned to Christ completely and were seeking in the direction of original or primitive Christian life, together with others. No Church, no sect, but an alliance of all believers!

It was in one of these meetings on March 4, 1907, that I heard Eberhard speak for the first time. He spoke about the words in the Letter to the Hebrews, chapter 10, "Since we have confidence to enter the sanctuary by the blood of Jesus . . . let us draw near with a true heart in full assurance of faith." It was in Else Baer's house, quite a well-to-do home. After this meeting he was surrounded by the listeners, asking him about this call and how it could be put into practice. I held back, but felt very much challenged. A short time later Eberhard told me that he had known from the first moment that we belonged together.

On the Sunday before Easter (March 24, 1907) we met again when Bernhard Kühn gave his addresses in the house of

the ophthalmologist. He was a small hunchback but a man full
of life and fire, who penetrated right into the hearts of his
listeners with his prophetic vision of God's future. "It does not
yet appear what we shall be, but we know that when He appears we shall be like Him, for we shall see Him as He is."
All who were present were deeply moved by this message. A
few spoke and witnessed to what Christ meant to them for
their whole future lives. I also stood up for the first time,
rather shyly, and said that from now on my life would belong
only to Christ!

After several such meetings (the series continued till March
27) Eberhard accompanied me home. We understood one
another very well in our common seeking. When taking leave
of me on the last evening, March 27, he asked me whether I
also felt that God had led us together. I answered, "Yes," and
felt myself bound from then on. I told my parents that I felt
as if I were engaged. The actual engagement took place on
Good Friday, March 29, when Eberhard called on my parents
to ask for their permission to marry me. They refused at first;
but then they allowed us to talk together. After we talked and
prayed together we felt ourselves engaged. My parents then
agreed to accept the engagement if Eberhard's parents also
would agree.

The time of our engagement was one of great joy and enthusiasm from the outset. We wanted to give our lives to Christ,
to save the lost, the down-and-outs, the sinners. We looked for
help and encouragement from our friends and associates in
the new groups already formed or in the process of formation.
We read together a good deal—from the Acts of the Apostles
and the letters of Paul, John or Peter. We also tried to study
the Revelation to John, but were able to understand but little.

Eberhard was able to come to Halle only for visits, as he was studying in Breslau for the semester. Because I was overstrained, but also because I was participating actively in the movement which was spreading all over Germany at the time, I did not return to Salzwedel. Further, I wanted to know the nature of early Christianity more deeply. We were very much concerned at the time to find deep unity with Christ and to establish a close relationship with those who had the same experience and were striving toward the same goal. We wanted to understand how the first Christians had really lived and what they believed. Through this the social problem and the question of the Church became very acute for us. We came to realize strongly to what an extent the life we had known was divided into classes and castes. How many people, including ourselves, enjoyed a position of privilege, not only in worldly possessions but also in an intellectual sense, a matter which does not appear so evident at first.

We tried to find clarity in all these things, and it was a special gift of our engagement period that we found ourselves so much at one in these struggles. The nine volumes of letters we exchanged while we were engaged contain a good deal of our recognitions, strivings and sufferings for what we had seen together.

In the first place, our parents on both sides were altogether unable to understand our revolutionary approach to the problem of social justice and that of the Church. It became clear to us that the "World Church" stands on a completely wrong foundation because it accepts children into membership in the Christian Church by right of birth instead of their taking this step through their own faith, which alone makes it possible to receive baptism. When this became clear a bitter struggle ensued in our families. They used every possible means of trying to prevent us from taking the step of baptism. (There is more about this in our engagement letters.) Added to this difficulty was the fear of my parents that I would influence and "infect" my sisters and my brother, as nearly all of them were deeply involved in the movement already.

The matter came to a head when Eberhard was disqualified from sitting for his first theological examinations because he did not want to serve the State Church. When this happened my parents were more upset than ever. "How can a man bind the life of a girl to his own if he makes no efforts to establish a sound economic basis for his future family?" This was indeed an attitude of utter irresponsibility in their eyes and in the eyes of those who were of the same mind.

Soon afterwards Eberhard was preparing for his Ph.D. examination at Erlangen, which he was to take at the earliest possible date. In this he was successful about a year later, on or about November 29, 1909. In spite of the many-sided responsibilities which were his at the time (he was a lecturer and student counselor), he passed with highest honors (*summa cum laude*). Although this did not mean that Eberhard had established himself in a secure financial position in any way, we reminded my father of the promise he had made us previously, that there would be no further obstacle to our marrying once Eberhard had passed the Ph.D. examination. He hesitated at first, but finally he did hand over my documents the same morning. This enabled us to go to the registrar and give notice of our intention to marry, a formality which had to be completed three weeks before the actual wedding. We chose the first possible date for this—December 20! At last I was to get out of this prolonged period of suspense and uncertainty; the sooner the better! They nicknamed me "The Flying Dutchman" in those times, from my maiden name, "von Hollander."

Well, everything came to a good end finally, although there

were quite a few upsets and disturbances. In spite of this it was given that the wedding could take place in the house of my parents, in a manner in keeping with our own convictions. Eberhard's parents and most of the family also took part in the wedding. My parents-in-law, too, had made objections, pointing out that we should build our marriage on a sound economic basis. We, however, wanted to put our common life entirely on the basis of faith. This faith has never let us down in any sphere of our lives.

During the first few months of our married life Eberhard held many public meetings, often jointly with Ludwig von Gerdtell. The latter lived in our home for about six weeks, during February and March 1910, I think. This was not always an easy arrangement, because of certain ideas of food reform he cherished and because of his whole manner and style of living. At that time, Gerdtell was holding meetings in the largest hall in Leipzig, the city where we had our first home. Small open-house meetings in our home resulted from these lectures, and they were attended by seeking people who asked many questions.

Eberhard himself traveled about a good deal, addressing meetings. Some of his topics were: "Jesus in opposition to the Church," "The suffering and enslavement of the masses," "Jesus as He really was," "Following Christ," "The Future of God." He spoke in public lecture halls, mostly in cities such as Halle, Berlin, Hamburg, Magdeburg, Erfurt, and so on. In this he was supported and financed by various groups which were part of the movement of that time.

During the early months of our married life I accompanied him on these journeys as often as I could. We experienced many an hour together when we felt powerfully the movement of God's Spirit among us. People, old and young, would break down under the weight of their guilt and wrong past and eagerly seek a new life. However, we also met with some struggles and conflicts in these meetings. For example, once a professor stood up and asked those who were assembled to leave the hall in protest, because Eberhard had attacked the existing World Churches, saying they were built on a wrong foundation.

Often we had people visiting our home for personal talks, which sometimes continued the whole day long. On many occasions I had to help in the case of women or girls who came. The question would arise frequently how we could seek and find a completely new way of life. Again and again we tried to find a way out in cases of need, by taking people into our home, especially children.

Once we experienced a great tragedy. After Eberhard had spoken in a meeting, an unknown woman handed him a letter. In the letter he was asked to come to the writer's home on the same evening. She wrote, "If I had not been present at your meeting tonight, all of us, my husband, our four children and I would not be alive tomorrow morning. This is our last hope." Eberhard hurried to the address given and met the following situation. The woman was married to a law student and they had four children. The man was absolutely unable to support his family. The wife traveled around from town to town working as a dressmaker and teaching dressmaking with new patterns, trying to keep the family's head above water. Now they could no longer find any meaning to their lives. They had decided to put an end to it all by shooting the whole family. Unfortunately this did happen later in another town. Only two of the children, whom we had taken in, escaped this abominable deed. The husband and the other two children were dead, the wife in the hospital with a bullet wound in her head. Eberhard visited her there. After we had received the news, he rushed for the next train and hurried to the place where it had happened and from there to the hospital. It was a horrible situation. He was cross-examined both by the police and the criminal court, who were eager to establish who committed the crime; the woman was still alive. This event, which took place in 1912, shook us and shocked us profoundly. We realized how little we were able to help, the way we were living then.

It was a very great joy to us that God gave us children. Emi-Margret was born on March 10, 1911 and Eberhard on August 18, 1912. To us this meant a confirmation of our marriage, and the growth of our children was a special gift to us.

In the spring of 1913, after Eberhard had held meetings in Halle, where we lived at the time, on the topic of "Following Christ," he was stricken by tuberculosis of the larynx and lungs. This threw all our plans into an upheaval. We found refuge in a little Alpine hut in the mountains of South Tyrol. Here our second son Heinrich was born on December 23, 1913. We experienced a quiet time of contemplation, of "breathing in," and studied many books and writings together. This meant a good deal for us; yes, it was a real gift never to be forgotten, and of great importance for our future lives. The quiet and rest in the Alpine mountains gave Eberhard healing and recovery from his serious illness. (The doctors had given him up. He had seven infected places in his lungs and two operations on his larynx.) As I had to look after a sick husband and two, then three little children, we asked my sister Else to come and help us. From this time on until her death in 1932, she was Eberhard's secretary, serving him and all of us in complete dedication.

How we experienced the wonders of nature there, the Dolomite Alps in their majesty and grandeur, the seasons of spring, summer, autumn and winter, the magnificent Alpine flora, the rising of the sun behind the mountains and the red glow of the mountain tops at its setting! For a long time to come after our return home, we continued to feel a deep longing for this experience of nature given to us during the eighteen months there, before the outbreak of World War I.

> Longing, deep longing, part pain and part joy,
> In the hearts of men, in the breasts of birds migrating.
> Down here all is empty and lonely and dull.
> I am longing for Home, my Jesus, for Thee.

As I said earlier, our reading and searching together for deeper clarity and greater light meant a special source of strength to us. During this period we also studied some old Anabaptist writings, including those by Hans Denck and Balthasar Hubmaier. This great movement had sprung up in Switzerland and in Tyrol, where it found its main center. Jakob Huter, the founder of the Hutterian Brothers, was born in Tyrol. (In 1937, accompanied by our Hutterian brothers David Hofer and Michael Waldner, I visited many of these old sites, places that had been so moved and had seen so many martyrs.) The first chapters of Eberhard's book *Innenland* were published during this time under the title "Greetings from the Mountains" in various magazines, as well as other articles.

The move to the mountains with the whole family had been a daring step taken in faith. We had no regular income and no certain assurances of support. Our parents' idea had been that Eberhard should stay in a sanatorium. For this they wanted to help us financially, and it had been their suggestion that the rest of the family should be divided up. Above all they felt there was a danger of infection, especially for our smaller children. We, however, had felt very strongly that we should not be separated during a time like this, as the doctors had given little hope for Eberhard's recovery.

This time of quiet came to a sudden and abrupt end. During the night before August 2, the first day of mobilization, we received a telegram summoning Eberhard to report to his reserve unit immediately. This came as a great shock, although we had been conscious of the possibility of war breaking out from the news which had reached us in our mountain retreat. We had no radio then. Eberhard left the same day in a military train full to overflowing, en route from Bozen to Halle. From there he was immediately pushed on eastward. We did not hear from him either. All traffic, mail, etc. had come to a complete standstill. Since we had gone to the Tyrolean mountains solely for Eberhard's sake, we—Tata (Else) and Luise, a young German girl who was staying with us at the time, and I— considered whether we should not make use of the first opportunity to travel home.

When the news reached us that Italy had broken her alliance with Germany, we left Bozen the same day, August 18 (Hardi's second birthday), leaving everything behind except for the bare essentials. We managed to get on an overcrowded train leaving for Innsbruck the following day. Nobody could tell us how we would be able to travel on from there. This journey, which could be made in one night by express train, took us a full six days. Still, our fellow travelers were friendly and helpful, as we were traveling with three small children. Emi-Ma was three years old at the time, Hardi just two and Heini seven months. When we finally reached my parents' home in Halle after this long journey, we received news the same evening that Eberhard had been discharged from the army as physically unfit for active duty, and that he would be arriving the same day. What a homecoming it was, and what a reunion!

During our whole trip everything had been in the grip of war. Transports of wounded soldiers were coming back from the front and cattle transports were going toward the front. At home, in the railway station, in the streets, nobody talked of anything but the war. Great enthusiasm was evident everywhere. "Germany is surrounded by enemies from all sides. We want to fight, we must fight for our just cause, die for it and carry through to victory!" This was our immediate impression.

Eberhard told us a different story. He had been in Thorn in Posen, and he did not see everything in quite such a rosy light. We had different feelings too when we looked around among the Christian circles which were so close to us. Husbands, brothers and sons were at the front. "What else can we do but go along with the general trend, fighting for the great and just German cause and praying for victory?" This was the prevailing feeling. Where was the faith once so strong in the circles close to us that the fellowship of faith, the alliance of all Christians, stood high above all nationalities and the patriotic love for one's own country? The hate against England was particularly strong, even among those who had experienced Christ. "We are German Christians, and God will give victory to our cause. May God punish England."

We lived in an atmosphere of this kind for about a year, in a small house at Dölau near a pine forest, not far from Halle, with our three little children; this was especially on account of Eberhard's health. Eberhard was busy writing his book *Innenland* ("Inner Land") with the subtitle, "The War, A Challenge to Inner Life." People, including some who called themselves Christians, said to him, "*Herr Doktor*, we are at war. We have no time for inner life!" Eberhard made regular trips to Halle and to other towns, as he had done before his illness, holding meetings and calling people to faith in a serious time. He always spoke against the prevailing war spirit. However, we had no clarity at that time as to how far our conscience would let us go to help the war effort; for example, whether we could do ambulance duty, and so on.

In 1915 we began a completely new period of our life together. Eberhard was asked to work with the Assistance Committee for Prisoners of War. His main task was in the literature department of the recently founded Furche Publishing House in Berlin. The whole organization was headed by Georg Michaelis, Undersecretary of State, who was the chairman of the D.C.S.V. (*Deutsche Christliche Studentenvereinigung,* or "German Christian Student Union"). As Eberhard had been both a member and director of this organization in Halle, he was asked to be an editor of the new monthly magazine of the D.C.S.V., *Die Furche* ("The Furrow"). The publishing house produced books, pamphlets and art reproductions for prisoners of war and wounded soldiers in the military hospitals. These publications often had a German nationalistic slant. For example, one was called *Der Heiland,* meaning "The German Savior." This was done, of course, to foster morale, to strengthen the will to hold out until the victory for "the just German cause" should be won. Everybody was expected to contribute his share toward this victory. It was simply taken for granted that the other side was fighting for an unjust cause.

The fact that Germany was surrounded by enemies on all sides and had to fight them all simultaneously weighed heavily on us all, and every German both wanted and felt obligated to give himself, his blood and life, as his own small contribution to the whole war effort. In the streets German flags were in evidence everywhere, on public and private buildings, as soon as a new victory had been won against Russia, England or Italy. Notices announcing the "heroic death" of the soldiers, as well as the lists of the wounded, were displayed publicly, causing great shock and sorrow to many.

As the months went by, food for the people became scarcer and scarcer, until finally it was completely insufficient. Bread, sugar, fat, meat and other items of food could be bought only with ration cards, and the quantities became smaller and smaller. At one time the weekly rations per person were as follows: 4 lbs. bread; 4½ oz. sugar; less than ½ oz. butter, and a little more margarine. Only rutabagas (a variety of turnip) could be bought without ration cards. Ersatz coffee and many other things were made out of rutabagas.

Because of all this, the situation reached the starvation point toward the end of the war. The morale of the people did not improve, especially when it became known that a good deal of inequality existed. Some who had money and connections were able to get hold of almost anything, while others were nearly perishing. Nevertheless all were expected to fight and give their lives for "the cause" on an equal basis. Some had all they wanted, while living in the very same house there would be others in great need, such as the caretaker's family. He after all was doing them the service of looking after the house, yet he was forced to let his children go to school hungry. They did not even have coal to make hot soup for the children, and their money was often not enough to buy even those items of food that were available on ration cards.

We heard that the same kind of inequality existed at the front and behind the front lines, yes, that there, where fathers and brothers were fighting, it was even worse. Officers lived in luxury, while the common soldier had to carry on with the barest minimum. Toward the end of the war we heard more and more expressions such as, "Equal food and equal pay, and soon the war will fade away," or, "Wait until they come back home. Out there they have learned how to steal." (Looting went by the name of requisitioning.) Naturally this did not help to raise the flagging spirit of patriotism.

During this period Eberhard paid frequent visits to army hospitals, where he had freedom to come and go as a student counselor. He was often extremely depressed when he came home from such visits. He told us of the suffering, the anguish, the tormented consciences of many soldiers, and about the whole war atmosphere with its atrocities.

During the later war years the voice of conscience was raised more and more audibly. "Is it possible for a Christian, yes, for a human being, to take part in this kind of mass murder?" "Is there any justice on this earth?" "What about the whole social order? How is it possible that all are fighting for the same goal, Germany's victory, and giving their lives for this, while at the same time such blatant contrasts continue? For instance, just compare the hospitals for officers with those for the common soldiers." Yes, the soldiers at the front were the most concerned of all, because their wives, mothers and children were living in such misery at home while they, their breadwinners, were fighting at the front. And at the same time others who had stayed at home were having a good time and could get what they wanted. We ourselves observed these very same conditions daily in our own house.

When the hope for a victorious end of the war, which had upheld the people, finally was shattered, a great sadness, a hopelessness and despair took hold of the masses. Before my eyes I can still see the people standing in groups in front of the posters proclaiming the conditions of the armistice. They cried out, *"Wir sind kaputt!"* ("We are finished!") Yes, nearly all had cherished the hope up to the last minute that the war would end in Germany's favor. The flags of victory which had been kept flying right to the end had strengthened this delusion. But now the truth was out. The Kaiser had abdicated and fled to Holland. (Why didn't he stay with the others, who kept their soldier's vow to the bitter end, fighting and dying "For God, King and Fatherland"?)

The army was retreating. More and more news became known. I will never forget the endless columns of grey, bearded, deeply saddened soldiers passing our house in those days, with their pieces of artillery and their field kitchens. They came home after four years in the front line. Nobody dared to say a word. Great sadness and mourning, disillusionment and fear of the future could be read on all faces.

# THE WIND BLOWS

ONLY A FEW DAYS later and the streets looked different again. Big trucks raced through the streets of Berlin, bedecked with the red flag—the flag of the revolution. This flag was taking the place of the black, white and red one—the colors of the old German Empire—everywhere, on the public buildings, even on the Imperial Palace. Many private homes hung out red flags too. Columns of men, still in their military uniforms, boldly marched through the streets of Berlin. It was November 9, 1918. Now all the pent-up suffering and hate of the oppressed people burst out. How many things had they not seen and heard! There was some sharpshooting with machine guns. Brother against brother! We could hear the *tac-tac-tac* and the rattle of the machine guns right in the center of Berlin, but also to the east and north of the city quite often, even daily. Other scenes gave us the impression that Berlin had gone mad. In the center of the city, in the Potsdamer Platz where it joins the Leipziger Strasse, we could see men with both legs shot away and only one arm left, cranking hand organs; everyone who passed by was drawn into a wild dance to their music. It was just crazy!

A few days later the new government was to be elected in the biggest hall of Berlin, Circus Busch. Masses of people pushed their way inside, Eberhard and I being part of the crowd. It was a deeply shocking experience when somebody from the crowd shouted, "Where was God in 1914? Were there any Christians at all then? The clergy of all the different Churches were right in it, too; they even blessed the weapons!" A Chinese got up and shouted, "We became converted Christians in our homeland, but what we have experienced here, what we have been taught—one Christian nation fighting the other, men killing one another—we have lost our faith which the missionaries brought to us. Christianity has become a mockery to the Hindus and Chinese!" This and similar things were said in this meeting and in others like it which we attended in those days. When the actual election took place, names were suggested from all sides, from the Democrats to the extreme left represented by Karl Liebknecht and Rosa Luxemburg, who had moved into the Imperial Palace. Finally the man agreed upon was Ebert, who was asked to lead Germany.

Something else happened in those days, something which had perhaps been in evidence already during the last period of the war. A great questioning began, mostly among the young people from all kinds of backgrounds, whether working class, artists' circles, atheists or Christians. "It cannot go on like this. After all, what is the meaning of life?" This questioning came to us also through the Furche Publishing House and the youth circles connected with it. Eberhard was asked to take part in youth conferences of the Free German Youth movement and the Christian Student Union.

The whole situation, all this seeking and searching, brought us into contact with a great number of people. We began to have weekly open-house meetings in our own home as a result. When the number of those attending grew to 80 to 100 people, we began to hold these meetings twice weekly. Those who attended were: members of the various branches of the youth movement, young people from Christian groups, anarchists, atheists, Quakers, Baptists, artists, and also representatives of the revivalist movement.

What did all these people have in common? Wasn't it just a great hodgepodge, a complete chaos? No. What made these people meet together was this single question: "What shall we do? It can't go on like this any longer." And there was nobody who was able to give a clear-cut answer. This is how it happened that we all came together as people united in one common search, one common quest. We were waiting and open for any kind of helpful word; and it came to us, too. Oftentimes we sat up together until after midnight, until finally, after a prolonged struggle, a word of help was given. Men like Tolstoi and Dostoevski spoke to our condition through their writings.

The Furche Publishing House had brought out a book at that time with the title *Die arme Schwester der Kaiserin* ("The Poor Sister of the Empress"). In one of our meetings Eberhard read a story from this book, "The Rachoff Case." It was the story of a young man from a wealthy home in Russia who is called by Christ and inwardly urged to give his life in service to the poor. He leaves his father's house, wanders about and meets much need and suffering among the people. Out of his love he tries to give help. Finally he is cast into prison and has to suffer much himself; he meets with a sad end.

We invited the author to attend one of our open-house meetings; we were full of anticipation that he would open up the way for us and show us what we should do. It was a tremendous disappointment when he said, "Yes, I wrote the book, and I was moved when I wrote this story, which is based on recorded facts. But I never said that I would do the same thing myself." All who were present were greatly disappointed; for they, like ourselves, were looking for a way of action. Words there had been enough; there had been an overabundance of sermons by the clergy of all denominations, who had also blessed the arms of war. What mattered now was action, not words.

During the year following the armistice, a great number of conferences and retreats were organized. By these means, those who participated, particularly from the younger generation, were seeking to find a direction for their future lives. First of all there was the D.C.S.V. Conference on the Frauenberg, a mountain near Marburg, at Whitsun, 1919. Here Eberhard was asked to speak to the students on the theme of the Sermon on the Mount. We have a report of this conference in our archives, containing reviews of Eberhard's address and telling of the effect it had on his listeners. This report was published in *Die Furche*. We quote from the words of Erwin Wissman by way of example.

> The focus of all that was said and thought was Jesus' Sermon on the Mount. Eberhard Arnold burned it into our hearts with a passionate spirituality, hammered it into our wills with prophetic power and the tremendous mobile force of his whole personality. This was the Sermon on the Mount in the full force of its impact, in its absolute and undiminished relevance, its unconditional absoluteness. Here there was no compromise. Whoever wants to belong to this Kingdom must give himself wholly and go through with it to the last! To be a Christian means to live the life of Christ. We are obligated by a burning challenge: the rousing summons to live, and the ominous warning, "He that takes the sword shall perish by the sword."

The discussions that followed were extremely lively, and from this conference a stream of life, a vision of the future, came into our open-house meetings. The fruits of this experience became more and more visible, until finally a new form appeared. Another conference was convened by the Christian student movement in August 1919. The main topic was, "What is the attitude of a Christian to war and revolution? Can a Christian be a soldier?" Eberhard's answer was a clear No.

A report of this conference says:

> Eberhard Arnold recognizes the necessity of the new birth, and he said that this belongs to the [Christian] proclamation. Jesus recognized the authority of the State, but He spoke of the Kingdom of God as something quite different. The Christian must be a perpetual corrective of the State—a conscience of the State and its legislative task, a leaven, a foreign body in the sense of a higher value; but he cannot be a soldier, an executioner or a police chief. It is our task to bear witness in word and deed and see to it that nothing in Jesus' words becomes confused. We must obey God rather than men! We must be a corrective element in this world!

These words of Eberhard's struck like lightning, and an animated discussion ensued. It was more than just an intellectual discussion; it was as if the very bottom had dropped out of things. Hermann S. contradicted Eberhard most vehemently. He as well as others represented that the State is "God's servant to punish evil and to foster good," as Paul expresses it. In a relative sense Eberhard agreed with this concept of the State as God's servant. But now was the hour to testify to the will of Jesus for His *followers*—a way of non-violence!

After this there was another conference in Saarow, Brandenburg, where the same theme was the center of the discussions and deliberations. Still another conference was held in Tambach in Thuringia in October. Here we experienced our first encounter with the Swiss Religious Socialists. It was here too that we met for the first time Karl Barth, who was one of the main lecturers. The testimony of the Swiss, especially that of Karl Barth, of the "God quite other than man," made a deep impression on the people there.

I remember a small incident which occurred at the end of the conference. The chairman, Otto H., a member of our movement, had said something to this effect to close the conference: "Let us go home now and consider everything we have heard. We will meet again next year and see whether God is still alive." There were roars of laughter at this from the Swiss. They felt his expression was wrong, for how can we little men want to see whether the *living God* is still alive? (Otto actually meant that God will surely be alive.) Otto felt offended and left the meeting. After he had been persuaded to come back, the Swiss made a public apology for their outburst of laughter. It can be seen from this incident what kind of atmosphere existed at that time.

At Eberhard's places of work the same kind of tensions existed. At this time he was literary director of the Furche Publishing House, general secretary of the Christian Student Union and assistant worker of the German student service for war prisoners. Opinions here were divided into two opposing camps. All were aware of the confusion prevailing among the youth, a result of the turmoil and suffering of the war years. There were those who wanted to lead the young people back on the beaten track of Church life and revivalist pietism. Others again, among them Eberhard, believed that the young generation was looking on public events with an entirely different eye as a result of the war and the revolution. They had learned a lesson from the blatant inequalities, the shirking of military duty, and the whole war psychosis which they had so painfully observed. They believed that they had to go an entirely different way, the way of which Jesus had spoken, the way of the Sermon on the Mount.

The attitude of the latter group came to expression in the publications of the Furche Publishing House and the manuscripts submitted, and resulted in a number of struggles and conflicts with the men of the "old" direction. At about this time we became acquainted with the people of the publication *Christian Democrat*, later *Das neue Werk* ("The New Work"). We grew closer and closer to these new friends, who were seeking to find new ways and were willing to go on them as we were. That which was old and rotten should not be a part of the new life!

Meanwhile the struggling and searching continued in our open-house meetings. The Sermon on the Mount was both our goal and our direction. However, there were other voices too which made themselves heard. Some said, "It is impossible to live up to this today! There will always be rich and poor. One can't cut out competition. Everyone has to see for himself how he can get along in life. Life is hard. What would happen if we permitted everyone to take advantage of us?" And against this, the words, "If someone wants to take your jacket, give him your coat also. Live like the lilies in the fields and the birds in the air. Have no enemies. Love your enemies. Do good to them!" Yes, all these conflicting things were said. To us, of course, came questions like, "What would you do if somebody were to carry off your big sideboard?"—"What would you do if somebody were to rape or kill your own wife in your presence?" and other similar questions.

Our circle had grown. Members of both the youth movement and the workers' movement had come to us as a result of the various conferences—young people who were not burdened by past experiences. The slogan which had been coined as early as 1913, that is, before the war, by the Free German Youth at the Hohe Meissner Mountain, was a living word among these young people urging them to action. It went something like this: "We want to be free to build up and determine our own lives in a truthful and genuine way." The workers' movement was fighting for liberty, equality and fraternity. "We know no differences. We know no enemies. All this is caused by the upper classes, and the simple people are then made to follow their example and do the same thing!"

Now we arrived at the question, "What then shall the new life be like which began to dawn upon us in the Sermon on the Mount?" Many suggestions were made in the circle. It became more and more unbearable to carry on in the old middle-class life. We discussed a number of possibilities—folk schools, cooperatives and land settlements of various kinds. Eberhard and I had the idea of buying ourselves a gypsy trailer, or even several, and traveling from village to village this way, from town to town, with our family and those who wanted to join us. We would make music, bring joy and help to people, and teach our children as we went along. We would travel without a destination, staying in a particular place only as long as our help was needed and accepted there by the widows, the children and the sick, whose destroyed homes we would rebuild. This idea found a good deal of response in many people.

A short time later, in the same open-house meetings, we read the accounts about Pentecost in Acts 2 through 4. We felt that here was the answer to our seeking and questioning. Community of faith, community of love, community of goods! "They had all things in common." Born out of the love energies of the first Christians! Perhaps there was to be an itinerant community in gypsy trailers or on foot. But we had to be messengers of a Church aflame with love.

We are like fires through the darkness burning,
And though we may burn but a single night,
Yet joy upon joy in wealth o'erflowing
And light to the land our fire has brought.

Now we were looking for actual possibilities. In the city? In the country? Our worker friends favored a settlement in the country which would give people like themselves a chance to visit us there, away from the industrial towns. We ourselves were contemplating a settlement in a city, in collaboration with the fellowship we had helped to create in Halle in 1907. This group was thinking of putting a large house, containing a big hall, at our disposal, right in the slum area of the town. Yet many obstacles would have to be overcome because of the overcrowded conditions prevailing in the cities and elsewhere at that time.

Eberhard traveled about a good deal looking for a suitable place. A letter by Georg Flemmig, a teacher from Schlüchtern, between Frankfurt and Bebra, pointed to possibilities in that region. His letter was a call, a challenge to the primitive Church. It showed us that groups who lived in the same spirit of expectation were to be found in every part of the country, and that the movement was not confined to our own circle. Eberhard traveled to Schlüchtern soon to get acquainted with the circle gathered there.

From Schlüchtern Eberhard looked around to seek possibilities for our new beginning. He visited the Ronneburg near Gelnhausen, an old ruined castle which would have to be completely rebuilt. A good friend of ours, Friedrich Wilhelm Cordes, a man of some means from Hamburg, sobered Eberhard's enthusiasm for this project considerably when he said, "How will you get people here who would be able to rebuild this place?" Yet Eberhard was much impressed by the spiritual history of the old castle. Here, in the time of Zinzendorf in the eighteenth century, a group of people had lived in community of faith and goods, and Zinzendorf, who was exiled from his own country, Saxony, on account of his faith, had participated in this. However, the Ronneburg plan was given up soon; yet we were to visit the castle often in times to come.

Two more conferences took place during this period, before our actual beginning. We had sent invitations to a number of interested and seeking friends to meet with us on the Insel Mountain in the Thuringian forest. I believe the actual place of meeting was Fröttstatt. From there we climbed the mountain with our rucksacks, our guitars and violins, singing and making music together. The people who met with us shared our own great concern—to create a new way of life.

It was good to be talking things over together in the midst of this wonderful scenery in the early springtime. Between meetings we sang together a good deal, old and new German folk songs, such as *Wie schön blüht uns der Maien* ("O lovely, flowering Maytime"), *Der Winter ist vergangen* ("Winter is past"), and others. We often sang the song about the blue flower which one must find deep in the forest, *Wir wollen zu Land ausfahren*:

> Let's walk in the open country,
> Over the meadows far,
> Out where the lonely summits
> Clear in their beauty are;
> List'ning whence blow the storm-winds chill,
> Looking what lands lie beyond the hill,
> Earth stretching wide and far.
>
> And deep in the wood there is blooming
> The tiny flower blue;
> And just to win this flower

> We'll travel the wide world through.
> The trees are a-rustle, the stream murmurs low,
> And he who to seek the flower blue would go
> Must be a wanderer too!

This song was particularly suitable for the youth movement of that period, which had left the old ways behind and had entered on the search for "the blue flower."

Everyone sensed that hidden behind and in nature lay a mystery: God. Most had not experienced God or had lost Him through the intoxication of the war. Here we felt something of a true quest for the unknown God and a sense of great reverence for Him when we were gathered together in nature, and in what we sang and experienced together.

> A quiet song, a peaceful song,
> A song so tender and fine,
> Like a cloudlet that over the blue sky sails,
> Like cotton-grass blown in the wind.[1]

Behind all this stood God the Creator, whose Name we did not dare to pronounce, because it had been misused so often. This experience of deep fellowship, of which I personally became a part in this way for the first time in my life, was a seeking, and at times more than a seeking, to experience God.

In the course of these conferences we not only experienced nature and the mystery hidden behind it. We also did some hard work and engaged in an eager search for a new possibility, a new goal in life. Separate groups were formed to tackle specific tasks, such as exploring ways and means to start a country school or a folk school, to create a social work center, etc. One group was especially concerned to consider the founding of a land settlement, and many participated in this.

[1] A verse from *Alle Birken grünen in Moor und Heid'* by Hermann Löns.

It was emphasized that man should return to nature, to farming and agriculture, as a basis for such a settlement.

Eberhard developed his thoughts on a future settlement and summarized them in an article, "The Fellowship of Families and Settlement Life," written at that time. He spoke of (1) farming and gardening, (2) school and education, (3) publishing and outreach, (4) a children's home to give special help to war orphans, (5) craft work. This vision found quite an echo, but most people saw its realization only in a far distant future.

At the end of this conference Marie Buchhold, who had helped start a women's community near Darmstadt, stood up and said, "There have been enough words. Let us see some action at last!" At this we parted from one another, firmly resolved to go into action now. This was the end of the conference. We descended the mountain with the joyful song on our lips, *Wann wir schreiten Seit' an Seit'*:

> When we're striding side by side
> And the songs of old are singing,
> Echoes from the woodlands ringing,
> Every heart in joy's believing,
> With us goes a new, new time!

The other conference I referred to as coming before our own beginning was the Whitsun Youth Conference at Schlüchtern in 1920. In conjunction with others we had invited keenminded young people from various groups to join us for this meeting. We left Berlin on a *Bummelzug* ("slow train") at five o'clock in the morning. It was the kind of train that stopped at every station. We traveled fourth class (since discontinued) because it was the cheapest way. We were due to arrive in Schlüchtern at eight o'clock in the evening. With us in the train were a number of people from the youth movement, the boys wearing peasant blouses and the girls simple dresses in bright colors. All carried violins and guitars with them. Our other traveling companions enjoyed listening to the beautiful songs of nature and hiking songs. They sat on the four benches along the four walls of the compartment, while we stood in the middle during the whole trip, since no other seats were available in this fourth-class section of the train.

When we arrived at our destination we climbed to the top of a hill where we lit our Whitsun fire, which shed its light far and wide over the whole countryside. The burning fire was a symbol for us of the burning up of the old and of hope for the coming of the new. We were thinking of the fire of which Jesus said, "I came to cast fire upon the earth; and would that it were already kindled!" It was all as real as if Jesus himself were speaking to us.

We sat under the lofty beech trees and listened. There were talks given, leading to discussions. After these, with our heads humming, we would dance together. It was folk dancing we did, real community dancing. "The people are dancing in a circle." We also sang folk songs, songs of love and of nature. We would sit around on the ground forming a large circle, the girls with garlands of daisies in their hair, the boys in their shorts and peasant blouses. Outward formality and convention were cast off. We simply felt as men among men. There was a spirit of joy, a spirit of true comradeship alive among us. This kind of thing one must experience personally. Our dances were, I must say, a truly religious experience, as Eberhard put it in one of his poems:

> Spirit-gripped,
> Move as one.
> Circle round,
> Center bound!

Between meetings we cooked our meals on open fires in the beech wood. Everyone unpacked what provisions he had in his rucksack, and all shared the simple meals, gathered in little groups around the cooking pot.

What concerned us throughout these Whitsun days was our urge to carry something new into the world, to blaze a trail for the Kingdom of God, the message of peace and love. Francis of Assisi, with his love for men and animals, had much to say to us.

One morning the English Quaker John S. suggested to us to have a Quaker meeting. "The Germans still talk far too much." He began by explaining the true significance of a Quaker meeting to us. We were to sit together in silence for quite a long time, perhaps half an hour or longer, in order to listen to the Spirit, to the voice of God. A few seconds after John had ended, an elderly professor from Frankfurt rose to his feet and made quite a long speech. Thereupon John stood up and said, "Hush." The professor reacted in quite a touchy way. "You are very intolerant," he said to John. We all burst into laughter!

The topics we discussed were of deep concern to all of us. Above all we were concerned with the experience of Pentecost two thousand years ago and its consequences ever since. We talked about the "new life." The question of *Eros* and *Agape* (love, human and divine) was another topic we discussed. We all felt that something was breaking in upon us, that something of the Spirit of Pentecost was at work among us.

One day we hiked to the health reform settlement called Habertshof, near Elm. We wanted to get an impression of what the "new life" might look like. We town folk were deeply impressed by the simple life of these people up there on a hillside, above all by their complete lack of pretension, their plain peasant garb in the style of the youth movement. This impression was especially deep with those of us who wanted to make a real new beginning. Eberhard and I felt that our own life in the future should have a similar outward form. This settlement was begun by Max and Maria Zink from Swabia, a year before our own new beginning got under way.

While sitting together in the evening hours, we liked to sing Matthias Claudius' song, *Der Mond ist aufgegangen* ("The moon has gently risen"), and we never ended without singing our "Schlüchtern song," *Kein schöner Land*. On one occasion about a year later, after we had sung this song standing in a circle to close our meeting, the last verse was added spontaneously by Eva Öhlke on the way home.

> Brothers, we know the bond that binds:
> Another Sun for us now shines!
> In it we have our life, towards it we always strive—
> The Church of Life.

After taking leave of all who had been with us during this conference, Eberhard and I, together with some young people, took a walk to the near-by village of Sannerz. We had been told that a fairly large brick house was standing empty there. It belonged to a certain Conrad Paul who had built it with the dollars he had earned in America. It took us about two hours to reach Sannerz, as we took a route over the hills and also rested on the way. Our first stop was in the little village inn. We were well received and treated to some good food. We talked with the landlord and soon became acquainted with the whole history of the village and of its people, including the story of Conrad Paul in all its details! We went across to have a look at Paul's red brick house on the other side of the road. This building was to become a significant spot for us and for many other people later!

Conrad Paul was friendly and accommodating. The house seemed very suitable for our purpose, with its fifteen rooms, kitchen, and a number of attic rooms which could be remodeled for dwelling purposes. There were some cattle sheds, pigsties and poultry houses, a fine sizeable orchard and even some fields suitable for farming. The whole place impressed us as somewhat too "middle-class" compared with the Habertshof, which had seemed to us so much more appropriate for the simple life we were intending to enter upon. But in those times there was not too much choice. Farmers liked to keep their places for themselves because of the advantages of agriculture in a Germany too poor to be able to import much. Our difficulty with Paul was that though he seemed willing to rent out or sell the place, he would never say what payment he wanted.

We returned to Berlin with this question unsolved; yet we were planning for an early move. We began to pack, although we did not yet have a definite place to go to. As it happened so often in our lives, we had to act in simple faith and trust that we would be guided clearly in what we did.

# BEGINNING AT SANNERZ

THE SITUATION with the Furche Publishing House had become increasingly difficult. Articles and manuscripts which we and our friends found particularly challenging and suitable for publication were not at all appreciated and even turned down by those in influential positions who represented the old, traditional way of thinking. As a result there was a continual struggle, a most frustrating situation for us at a time when the need of the hour and the Spirit moving abroad were calling us to a new task. It was just then that our friends at Schlüchtern asked Eberhard to take charge of the *Neuwerk Verlag* ("New Work Publishing House") they were planning to start, although the necessary funds had still to be raised to make this possible.

No, there was no financial basis of any kind either for our community settlement or for the proposed publishing house, when we decided to turn our backs on our past lives and to start afresh in full trust. Our well-meaning friends shook their heads; what an act of rash irresponsibility for a father of five little children to go into complete nothingness, just like that! Frau Michaelis, the wife of the former Chancellor of the Reich, called upon me and offered her help to me and the children in case my husband should really take this "unusual" step. After her conversation with me she said about me elsewhere, "*She* is even more fanatical than *he* is. Nothing can be done!"

Our departure on June 21, 1920, came about very suddenly. Our youngest girl Monika, then two years old, was very sick and weak as a result of the war need and in particular the lack of nourishing food. The same was true of Hans Hermann, four years old, our youngest boy, who, like Monika, was born during the war years. Both children had all but lost their ability to walk. When in addition to this Monika became ill with a gastric infection, our pediatrician advised that we move immediately to the country with the little girl, so that she could get fresh milk, eggs, honey and good flour. We decided to send a telegram to the owner of the village inn in Sannerz, announcing our arrival for the next day.

Thus Eberhard and I traveled to Sannerz with our little Monika early on Sunday morning. It was the day of the summer solstice. Our four other children followed a few days later, accompanied by our helper Suse Hungar and a Salvation Army sister, Luise Voigt. Both had volunteered to go with us, at least for a time. My sister Else had to stay behind for a longer period as she was busy winding up our affairs with the Furche Publishing House. Friendly Mr. Lotzenius, the innkeeper, had three little rooms ready for us during the summer, which he had been using for his harness making and for apple storage during winter. We had set our hopes on Conrad Paul's house on the other side of the road, set further back from the road. The owner, however, hesitated. To begin with, he was not even sure whether he wanted to sell or to lease. He had hopes, too, that if he left us in a state of suspense he would get more for the place eventually.

Some money had been offered to us—a matter of 30,000 marks (which still had some value in those days)—for the purpose of founding a "primitive Church-community." The donor was our friend Kurt Wörmann of the Hamburg-America

Line. We planned to sell our life insurance policy, too, although this would not bring us much in cash. We were determined to burn all our bridges behind us and put our trust entirely in God, like the birds in the sky and the flowers in the field. This trust was to be our foundation, the surest foundation there is to build on!

After several weeks had gone by we finally reached an agreement with the owner of the house. We were to sign a rental agreement for a period of ten years, and buy all the farm equipment and furniture on the place and all the live-stock, consisting of four cows, several goats, pigs and chickens. For this we had to pay 30,000 marks down, including the rent for a year in advance, dating from the fall of 1920 to the fall of 1921.

Right from the start the summer brought us a good many guests. Most of them had to sleep on straw in the barns of the farmers nearby. The greater part of them came from the youth movement, of course, from all its various groups and camps. It was difficult to find work for these young people, though. The only job on hand was the gathering and chopping of firewood from the forests around, for use in the kitchen and laundry.

Little by little we were able to take possession of the New Work House, as we had named it. At first three rooms had become available on the ground floor at the front, which we used for general offices and for the publishing work. Finally, shortly before Christmas, during Advent time, we had the use of the whole building, as we had been able to get to-gether all the money due. Filled with great enthusiasm we sang one Advent song after another, such as *Willkommen, du selige Weihnachtszeit* ("Welcome, holy Christmastide"), *Kling, Glöckchen, klingelingeling* ("Ding dong, little bell, ding dong ding"), *Tochter Zion, freue dich* ("Daughter of Zion, rejoice!"), *Macht hoch die Tür, die Tor' macht weit* ("Lift up your heads, ye mighty gates"), and other German carols. A new song was given to us during this time. We sang it for the first time at Else's window on her birthday, December 13. It was an expression of our community experience: *Wir sind im heilgen Warten zu Haus* ("In holy waiting we're at home"). At six o'clock every morning we would gather around the kitchen fire where the oatmeal was cooking. We would sit there in silence listening, all of us who had joined forces to enter on this new life together, after the numerous summer guests had left us. A powerful spirit of expectancy was living in us; yes, it seemed to us as if the Kingdom were to break in any day! We who were living in community, together with those who came to stay with us, all shared in this experience of expectancy. We did not know what the next day would bring.

We went to work now on the publishing, the office work, small-scale farming, the education of the children (including teaching school), and the daily housework. There were seven of us at that time who began this life in community and wanted this kind of life. These things were of special importance to us: simplicity and plainness; poverty, for the sake of Christ. How could we, who wanted to serve love and share in the suffering of the people in those post-war years, still keep anything for ourselves? That is why we shared everything in common, giving away all we had or owned to the brothers and to those who wanted to serve the same Spirit with us.

Another matter of great importance to us was chastity, the purity of each individual, and marriage as a symbol of the unity of God with the Church. We were fully conscious that all this was possible only through faith in Christ and through

giving ourselves over to Him. It was a joy to us to be allowed
to have a part in this!

During the winter we did not have so many guests, which
made it possible to have a time of deep gathering together.
But as soon as spring was upon us, already in March, many
guests began to arrive. Young people, hiking in the beautiful
countryside to experience nature, came to visit us. Who had
money for train travel in those days anyhow? Nobody wanted
it either. During this first summer some 2,000 guests came,
staying with us at least one night. Among them were students,
Free Germans, members of Christian groups, *Wandervögel*,[1]
anarchists, atheists, people who had turned their backs on the
existing order of things and did not even want to use coal or
tools, since these were produced at the expense of the workers
in mines and factories and made those rich who had not done
any work themselves. Nearly all these people were concerned
with community as the solution—the community of the people,
the fellowship of nations, a new relationship to nature and to
mankind as a whole! Union with God and with the Church-
community of Christ! We used to talk together until the late
hours of the night and the small hours of the morning. Many
times the arguments became heated, but usually we were able
to end on a harmonious note. Often we would end by having a
quiet dance, moving around in a circle, singing together *Tanzt
das Volk im Kreise, rundinella rula, tanzt nach alter Weise*
("The folk are dancing in a circle together, rundinella rula,
dancing to an old tune").

There were moments in our gatherings with guests when
something would come to us, as it were, something which did
not come from us, nor from the people who were visiting us.

[1] The name of the original German youth movement, meaning "birds
of passage."

This was especially true with people who were burdened more than most, or tormented by demonic powers. Eberhard on one occasion told about this in the following words.

Among us, those who were living together and those who came to share in this experience, the Holy Spirit brought us face to face with the presence of God, in our gatherings and meetings. The rooms in Sannerz and at the Rhön Bruderhof[2] were filled with a power in those early days, a power which did not originate from us who were living there, nor from those who were our guests; it was a power coming from God which visited us. It was an invisible power surrounding us. In this way we were able to understand Pentecost as the rushing wind of the Spirit visiting the expectant Church with the Holy Spirit. This wonderful mystery brought the Church into being. Here no will of one's own or word of one's own could be spoken or added, not even the word of a so-called leader or of a so-called opposition. The voice comes from the cloud and man is silent. However, this does not mean in any way that only those who confess Christ, who confess that they are converted or reborn Christians, are touched by the cloud. The very opposite is the case. We experienced again and again that the hidden Christ becomes revealed through men who insist that they have no faith. Christ visits all men, long before they have found unity with Him. We believe that the light of Christ illuminates every man who comes into this world.[3]

There are other instances where Eberhard writes about this period. For us who experienced this time of our first beginning, of our first love, this will always remain unforgettable. This

[2] *Bruderhof*: a place where brothers live.

[3] *Eberhard Arnold*. Rifton, N.Y.: Plough Publishing House, 1964, pp. 5–6.

expectation was very much alive among us. Even today we meet people in North America who, during this first period among us, experienced an impact which had an effect on their whole future lives. Also in Germany we met and still meet such people today.

It is quite clear, of course, that nobody can live from the past. Yes, today too the Spirit lives, calling men as in the times of John the Baptist. "Repent, for the kingdom of heaven is at hand!" Jesus calls men to follow Him, to leave everything in search of the one, the only precious pearl. Here and there this is happening now. But for everyone who does this, whether today or in the past, the beginning time, the time of the awakening of the first love, will always be of very special significance, and in weak times we will have to turn back to it again and again.

During this early period we experienced very strongly that men and women who seemed to have lost all faith as a result of the war and the revolution, now for the first time experienced God the Creator behind and in nature. From the experience of nature, from the blowing of the wind, they came to experience the Spirit, the Holy Spirit, whose will it is to bring God close to us. Frequently only in this way did people find Christ as the one true Way, as the Light who illumines the way for us men, Christ who Himself is the Truth!

However, there also was a good deal of opposition among the guests. Vegetarianism played a large role in this. Oh yes, there were many fanatics too, who wanted to eat nothing but raw vegetables or fully ripened fruit. A certain young friend of the movement would not eat anything at all any more, and in the end died of starvation.

It was clear to us from the beginning that we did not want to be the founders of a work of our own. Community can never be founded; it can only be given as a gift of the Spirit. We simply wanted to live as brothers among brothers, and take into our midst everyone who wanted the same thing. It showed itself again and again, however, that people who wanted to follow their own ideas were not fit to go this way. There were clashes in the daily life, in the discussions, even in the inner meetings. One or another simply could not stay, but had to leave. Hardly ever did it happen that anybody had to be sent away; the spirits separated out, though this did not always happen so quickly. During the day we would work. The evenings belonged to the guests, to the talks with them. Yes, as I mentioned earlier, the encounters often were quite heated, until something would break in among us which simply did not come from us and which would bring everyone to silence.

This was a time which perhaps could only come as a sequel of great shocks, such as war or revolution. All traditions had collapsed and become shattered. Our house was full to over-flowing with guests—up to two thousand during the first year! There were strange characters among them.

The guest who most impressed us was Hans Fiehler, who called himself "Hans-in-Luck." He wore a red woolen peaked cap, a red waistcoat, and shorts. On his back was written in bold letters, Hans-in-Luck. He traveled through the country with two violins; one was a good Italian one which he had acquired on one of his trips to Italy; the other was a tin one which he had obtained from some gypsies. He also had four ocarinas which he called the "great-grandmother," the "grand-mother," the "mother" and the "child."

When he entered a village or a town playing his ocarina, he would be followed by a large crowd of children. He always had something to say, always had a message to proclaim.

When he had gathered the children around him in the town or village square he would tell them a story about Heaven and earth, about men's future and that of the whole creation, that in times to come the whole earth would be like Heaven! Yes, in those times nearly all of the children had experienced something of the terrible war. They knew hunger and want and many even had lost father or mother or both during the war. He would form a circle with them and they would sing together,

> Let our hearts be always happy,
> Full of thanks and full of joy,
> For the Father up in Heaven
> Calls us His own children dear.

> Always joyful, always joyful
> For the sun shines every day,
> For the way of life is full of beauty:
> Joyful let us be alway.

Hans-in-Luck regarded Sannerz and the Sannerz house as a kind of home for himself and stayed with us for quite long periods of time. "Why," he would say, "do we always speak of the good old times? Why do we say, 'Once upon a time,' instead of 'One of these days it will be'? Why do we say '1920, 1921,' etc.? Why not '80 or 79 before the year 2000'?"

In 1924 he, together with the children, planted the "Tree of the Year 2000" in the meadow of our house in Sannerz, a lime tree. We all danced around it singing one of his childlike songs,

> When the Zeppelin comes again,
> When the Zeppelin comes again,
> Seventy-six before two thousand,

> It will fly and rumble 'round
> Sannerz house with much big noise.
> When the Zeppelin comes again . . . .

Or he would get us all, adults and children alike, enthused to march through the village with paper lanterns, and we would sing together, to the accompaniment of musical instruments, *Durch das Tor der neuen Zeit*:

> Through the gateway of the age,
> On we march with singing!
> Before us lies the great, wide world—
> Will our hopes come true at last?
>
> Up and down, and down and up,
> All our songs are ringing!
> Walls so high can't hinder them—
> Echo brings them back again.
>
> Through the gateway of the age
> In multitudes we're marching,
> Through the world so wonderful—
> In our hair, wild flowers gay.

His message about the Kingdom of God was meant very seriously. The song, *Menschheitseiszeit war geworden* ("Dismal, drear dawned mankind's ice age") came to us quite spontaneously, and we joined in when he played and sang. All of us were deeply stirred.

Several times Hans-in-Luck came into conflict with the authorities. During one summer he had rented an observation point, a tower-like structure, in the Harz Mountains, and worked as a tourist guide; he also sold souvenirs to those who came. On one occasion he left the observation point at lunch time and fixed a verse on the door:

Hans-in-Luck his tummy fills;
Do the same—beyond those hills.

When he returned he found a whole crowd of people there, smoking and drinking. Hans-in-Luck felt in them no respect for his "new world" atmosphere. He got angry, struck a match and set fire to the building. He was put in jail for a few days as a result, and wrote to us from his cell, "From the little attic room of a *Wandervogel.*[4] I have been locked up here for a few days and am sending you many heartfelt greetings."

Another time he helped the very poor of a certain large city to a good, substantial warm meal. In 1924 there was the inflation and many people were starving. So one day Hans-in-Luck went to one of the army generals and made the following proposal: Take your army field kitchen to the city and feed the poor people there, for this will be a good way to restore your prestige. I'll stand by and make a film of it all. And this really came off! Hans-in-Luck stood there with his camera and kept commanding the general, "Stand up smartly!"— "Serve it out yourself!" and so on. And then, when everything had been served out, Hans-in-Luck opened his camera and, lo and behold, there was no film in it! But fortunately for him the people were all on his side and so he got away with it all right.

Our house at Sannerz looked rather shabby from having so many people live in it, and so one day the landlord came and demanded that we should repaint it. But of course we had no money to pay for such work. Now just at that time two guests were staying with us, Hans-in-Luck and another man, and they said they would do the work if we would buy the paint. And then something really did happen! Downstairs

[4] "Migrating bird."

in the front hall they painted a big picture of the rising sun
and of someone ringing a bell,

> Bim, bam, bom:
> Spring of the nations, come!

And there on the staircase wall was a picture of the whole
household dancing and skipping after Eberhard who led them
gaily onwards and upwards. Everyone found a picture of himself—even the geese had not been forgotten! On another
wall were painted the notes of the song,

> Let our hearts be always happy,
> Full of thanks and full of joy,
> For the Father up in Heaven
> Calls us His own children dear,

with several children dancing round. We had no idea that
he had meant to do anything like this. While he was at work
some well-to-do visitors arrived and, looking at his picture,
asked him, quite astonished, "Where do you come from?"
The answer was, "From the lunatic asylum." It was no wonder
they inquired anxiously afterwards, "Whatever kind of a man
have you got there?"

Many years later, in 1939 or 1940, we read a book about
the resistance to Hitler in which it was said that Hans Fiehler
had been imprisoned by his brother, the mayor of Munich, and
tortured for his belief in future peace. After the war I wrote
at once to friends in Munich and we tried to trace him, but
it seems that Hans-in-Luck had disappeared, having suffered
the fate of many others who raised a protest at that time.

Other strange people came to visit us. There was an opera
singer, for instance, who sang to us for a whole evening, while
everyone listened. Another time a whole family turned up,

each member dressed like a particular wildflower from the
forest. "We come from the woods; we live in the woods; we
will return to the woods!" That was all they would say. Another
young man with a beautiful voice sang to us during one supper-
time, "With their twigs the trees are bowing; dear God is
striding through the woods."

Tramps also visited us from time to time, tipsy or drunk.
They were attracted by the music and the singing. Everyone
was welcome, and we tried to concern ourselves with each
one who came. In this way our Karl G. came to us one
day—drunk, but very much attracted by what he experienced
and saw. "I cannot stay with you," he said, "I am a wicked
man. What have you done to me?" After a lot of encouragement he tried to venture into a new life. He shared with us
the whole story of his life, a very sad story of how he came
to be a tramp. He was an alcoholic, never able to hold out
longer than three months at a time without drinking. Then
he would go away, and when he came home completely drunk,
he would ask our forgiveness and promise to mend his ways.
"I am not worthy to stay with you!" he would say. This went
on until the time of Hitler. Then came a time when he stayed
away altogether, and we never heard from him again.

Our life in community was a very joyful one, filled with the
expectation of a new future. This was especially so during the
first two years. Every day that we were able to live together
in community was a great day of celebrating, truly a festive
day! Everything that happened was used as an occasion to
celebrate. When we had bought a cow or a goat, for instance,
we would decorate it with wreaths of wild flowers and lead
it through the village, singing together. Whether we picked
up stones and rocks from the fields we had rented, whether
we hoed beans, peas or potatoes, or whether we preserved

fruit and vegetables or stirred jam — all of these occasions were opportunities for celebrating and for experiencing fellowship together. Everybody joined in, even those who were overburdened with work in the office because of the many books we published during those first years. Everybody wanted to share in the common work.

Among the books published during this time were the following titles: Tolstoi, *Religiöse Briefe* ("Religious Letters"); Joan Mary Fry, *Das Sakrament des Lebens* (a translation of *The Sacrament of Life*); Goldschmidt, *Die Rassenfrage* ("The Problem of Race"); Zinzendorf, *Über Glauben und Leben* ("On Faith and Life"); Blumhardt, *Das Reich Gottes* ("The Kingdom of God") and *Die Nachfolge Christi* ("The Following of Christ"); *Junge Saat: Lebensbuch einer Jugendbewegung* ("Young Seed—A Book of the Youth Movement"), a collection of vital articles, edited by Eberhard Arnold and Normann Korber; Georg Flemmig, *Dorfgedanken* ("Village Musings") and *Hausbacken Brot* ("Homemade Bread"); *Legenden* (a little book of legends), edited by Fritz Schloss. In addition, we published the monthly magazine, *Das Neue Werk*.

When I think back to these times and their movements, during this period following the First World War, I feel it was a foretaste of what we can expect in a much greater and more perfect measure in the future of the Kingdom of God. This was so in our life in Sannerz, and perhaps just as much at the Rhön Bruderhof. Often I almost shiver, but also feel a sense of deep joy and thankfulness when I remember those days. Something that came from eternity was living among us, something that made us oblivious of the limits of time and space. Thus miracles, as one may perhaps call them, were experienced among us in a quite natural way. All this happened in spite of us, as it were, in spite of our insufficiencies and incapabilities.

It is difficult to tell about such events. Often it happened quite simply and unobtrusively in our meetings that demonic powers had to retreat; that sick people became well again, almost unnoticed; that things happened which simply cannot be explained by men. In those times, times of expectation, we did not regard such occurrences as unusual at all. Everything that happened to us in those days seemed very natural to us at the time. Eberhard said to me once, a short time before he died, "God gave much to us, but He would have given more if we had had more strength."

Again today we are standing in such a time—a time before a storm, before a thunderstorm, before great events in the world at large. What shall we do? What is most needed in the world today is that true unity and brotherliness be actually lived among men. This is the greatest miracle; then the light on the candlestick can shine and illuminate all men. One does not light a candle to hide it under a bushel!

Our special holidays, Christmas, Easter and Whitsun, were celebrated in a very beautiful way. These events actually accompanied us throughout the whole year, not only on those specific days. Nevertheless, every one of these holidays was celebrated very intensively. This was so particularly at the time of Advent.

Almost every year we would rehearse a Christmas play together. With this we would go from village to village. First of all we would decorate the village hall with spruce branches to make the place suitable for the message of the play. Conditions were primitive. The rooms used for changing into our costumes were unheated even though it was winter, and the hall in which we were to play was heated for only an hour

beforehand by burning wood which we had to fetch ourselves
from the forest first! We never charged for admission, remem-
bering Jesus' words, "Freely ye have received, freely give."
We simply would place an empty sack at the door of the
hall, and into this the poor Rhön peasants deposited anything
they could afford to give—a piece of ham, a sausage, a loaf
of bread, and so on. After walking home, usually through deep
snow, we would enjoy a wonderful festive meal late in the
night, prepared from these gifts; a rare treat!

Often on Christmas Eve we would walk into the forest
together. There, in a spot well-sheltered from the winds, several had decorated a little spruce with candles beforehand. We
formed a circle around the tree and sang our old and newly
discovered Christmas carols and songs. Otto Salomon's *Seht,*
*im Osten wird es hell* ("Lo, a light is in the East") and
Eberhard's *Weihenacht, du Nacht der Nächte!* ("Christmas
Night! O Night of nights") were given to us in those days.
Eberhard's song expresses so much of what we experienced
together:

> Make us poor, just as Thou wert,
> Jesus, poor through Thy great love!

After the Christmas message had been proclaimed, everyone
took a lighted candle from the tree and we walked down the
Albing Mountain in procession. Each one would protect his
candle from the wind, and if one was blown out, it would
be rekindled from another. This for us is a symbol of brotherly
life.

During this period the silent Nativity scene was given to
us also. Eberhard was Joseph; I represented Mary. In those
days we did not carry a baby or a doll to represent the Christ
Child. We just held a bundle in which was a bright light, as

a symbol of the light that came into the darkness of this world. Little angels were placed around the crib, each one holding a lighted candle. Then came the shepherds, followed by the kings, who put their crowns at the feet of the Child. Frequently a great throng of people followed to pay homage to the King.

This Nativity scene has become well-known in our Bruderhof communities. As often as possible we chose the simplest cattle shed for it. At times we had nothing but this silent crib scene on Christmas Eve; the sharing of the presents and all the joy for the children followed the next day. At one time many years later, in Paraguay, we had a very impressive celebration on the morning of December 25. Very early, at three o'clock, the whole community was awakened by the sound of musical instruments and singing. Within a few minutes all had assembled and, walking behind the musicians playing violins, recorders and guitars, we went to the cattle shed, still in complete darkness. Here we stood before the Nativity scene and sang many songs. Then all of us, led by Mary, Joseph and all who had taken part in the scene, walked to the dining room, which was decorated with flowers and greenery, with a pyramid adorned with burning candles, like a Christmas tree, in the center. There we took our breakfast together and sang a great number of Christmas songs.

During the early years we were particularly fond of the song, *Sag Gott, warum man dich hier findt? . . . Aus lauter Lieb allein!* ("Tell, O God, why art Thou found here? . . . For pure love alone!") Actually, each year Christmas songs and carols were discovered quite afresh and were sung as if they were new ones. The song, *Gelobet seist Du, Jesu Christ* ("Praise to Thee, O Jesus Christ"), with the verse,

> The eternal light now enters here,
> Gives the world a new light clear.

> It shines out in the midst of night
> And makes us children of the light,

sounded like the music of the spheres when sung in Bach's arrangement—like a choir from Heaven.

Another year we were especially fond of the song, *Ich steh' an deiner Krippe hier* ("Beside Thy cradle here I stand"), for all its verses were full of meaning for us. The same is true of *Kommt und lasst uns Christum ehren* ("Come, give now to Christ all honor"), which was sung usually at the end of a meeting. Then Eberhard would take my arm and we all would walk through the whole house together and around the Bruderhof, singing.

All of us, including the children, loved very much the song, *Zu Bethlehem geboren* ("To us in Bethlehem city"). It was Fritz Kleiner's favorite song. In this way something new was added each year which had a particular meaning for us. One Christmas time we rehearsed the Play of the Virgins, a play about readiness. We played this in a good number of villages, and the audience was particularly impressed. *Heilig, heilig, heilig ist der Herr Gott Zebaoth; und alle Lande sind seiner Ehre voll* ("Holy, holy, holy is the Lord God of Hosts; and all the lands are full of His glory") is the concluding chorus of this play, sung when the five wise virgins enter the gates of Heaven. On July 26, 1933, Eberhard's fiftieth birthday, we repeated this play at home, for the community, and it had a great deal to say to us all.

In our early days I was very much impressed by our rehearsals; they were like inner meetings! We were particularly restrained in the use of words and rejected all religious terms unless their use in the spoken word or in songs was born out of a complete reverence for the holy object. Not only the adults, but also our children, were most sensitive during re-

hearsals of such plays and helped guard the atmosphere. Even
our two youngest ones, Hans Hermann and Monika, simply
would not stay at a rehearsal if it was not "nice." Naturally,
the children also produced their own little plays among themselves, and did so wholeheartedly. In the same way they were
very fond of their childlike Christmas songs.

There was something very special in this early time when the
children (as early as 1921 underprivileged children came to
us) were so much a part of the experience of the whole community. They were aware of many things that were going on,
as we realized in later years, even though they did not
understand everything.

Easter was always a special time for us. During Holy Week
we would gather around the events of two thousand years ago,
and on Holy Thursday we usually held a meal together for
which a lamb (actually a kid goat) would be prepared.
Probably many know the songs, *Bei stiller Nacht* ("By quiet
night") and *Da Jesus in den Garten ging* ("When Jesus went
into the Garden"). Good Friday was observed for the most
part as a quiet day for each one individually, after the story
of Good Friday had been read to us in the morning. On Saturday we would assemble in silence only at the hour of Jesus'
burial. Often we sang only this one song, *O Traurigkeit, o
Herzeleid*:

> Oh sadness, oh suffering of heart,
> Shall we not lament?
> God the Father's only child
> Is carried to the grave.
>
> Oh greatest need,
> God himself is dead.
> On the Cross He died,

> Thus gaining for us
> The Kingdom of Heaven
> Out of love.

Easter Sunday was a very special day of celebration, because the evil power, sin, separation and death are overcome through the resurrection of Christ! Often we would climb up to the Weiperz Cross before daybreak, at three o'clock in the morning. Here a fire was prepared beforehand. After we had kindled it we walked around its flames, silently and slowly. Everyone to whom it was given would say a brief word. At the rising of the sun we sang all our beautiful Easter songs and the Easter message was read aloud.

These were very deep meetings, and even though all our children who could walk were taken along, there hardly ever were any disturbances, as they were completely included and absorbed by the experience we had together. Guests also were among us, especially from the youth movement. Because of their inner reverence for "that which lies behind it," as they themselves expressed it, they hardly ever disturbed in any way. Often they would jump through the fire with us, singly or in pairs, once the flames had died down. This was a language not in words but through an act that came out of an inner experience. Of spoken words there had been too many in times past!

Whitsuntide was regarded by us as "our feast" more than any other. For it was through Pentecost and the first Church in Jerusalem that we were called to this life. Not that we wanted to imitate anything. This cannot be done in any case; but what is of the Spirit should never be imitated at all. It is not right to say that a Church was founded by men. It is a matter only of the Spirit. It is possible to found an orphanage, a children's home, a nursing home; but a Church, never. And it is as impossible to found a Church alone as it is impossible to marry without a partner.

Our Whitsun conferences of 1920 in Schlüchtern and 1921 in Sannerz will always remain unforgettable to those of us who took part in them. There was something of an outpouring of the Spirit there that was to bear fruit later.

It was not the great feast days alone that reminded us of the greatest events in human history; rather, the experience of these three great facts—the birth of Christ, His death and resurrection, and the first outpouring of the Holy Spirit—was present among us throughout the year. For instance, at special occasions we would sing Christmas songs in the summer and vice versa. Nevertheless we did love the seasons of the year and their corresponding holidays and festive times very much.

The true and genuine outer form, as it comes into being through unity, through the feeling of being one, was very significant to us in our life together, whether it concerned the style of books and typography, the work of artisans and craftsmen, the way furniture and equipment or the clothes and dresses we wore were made. What we liked most was the simplest and plainest form. Whenever possible we wanted beautiful colors, all of them—like the colors of the rainbow which, put together, give us the beautiful white, the color of light, symbolized in the figure *one*. Everything had its inner significance.

Our early morning meetings at dawn had a deep meaning for us. Nobody would take part in them whose inner life was at the time not right in any way. At that time we wore rings; the women and girls wore a metal headband, the men a ring on the finger. Both were open, as a sign or symbol of belonging to the open circle. If anyone had the feeling that there was something wrong in his or her attitude, the ring or band was not worn.

We were led together very deeply during this time by reading aloud the First Letter of John. We began doing this during the Whitsun Conference of 1921. We all climbed up the Albing Mountain early in the morning before breakfast with our musical instruments. We wanted to be led and strengthened during the day ahead by the words of the apostle of love! No wonder, then, that the whole ensuing conference was concerned with the way and the freedom of love.

There was of course no lack of rather effusive elements. One morning during the days of Whitsuntide, Max S. stepped into our meeting and implored the Spirit of God to fall down upon us from the beech leaves above. "What's this?" someone cried out. "Is this the Spirit we want to ask to come to us?" There was considerable unrest among all who were present. On the way home there was a different atmosphere, as if something of the experience of these days had been lost. But soon all were meeting again, continuing in the common seeking.

During the following summer we had an incredible number of guests, including many from the working class. They challenged us in a meaningful way to give up everything not really necessary, everything "bourgeois," things we ourselves did not notice so much, for the sake of love to the poorest. Eberhard was very deeply impressed by all that these people gave to help us on the way we had chosen. This was the case especially because Eberhard had known Hermann Kutter and the Swiss Religious Socialists since 1912, when he and I had read such books as *Wir Pfarrer* ("We Ministers") and *Sie Müssen!* ("They Must!")

Among the workers who visited us during this time I want to mention Christel Girbinger, Bastel Hinterberger, Therese

Gruber and Paul Oberländer, all Bavarians. There were other visitors during this summer too, men like Theo Spira, who was very much impressed by early Quakerism, and the Swedish Nicolai Scheiermann, who came together with Dr. Buchholz from Soden-Salmünster. One day these two visited together with Martin Buber, I think. It happened to be just the day when Suse Hungar was to be baptized, as Heinrich Euler, a friend from the Baptist Youth Movement, who was to perform the baptism in our wood-spring, was staying with us at the time. Unfortunately Suse could not be persuaded to wait for a little while with her baptism in view of these important visitors. As a result we were absent with the whole household most of the morning, a situation which I am sure was not very helpful.

Another time Eugen Jäckh, a friend of the younger Blumhardt, came for a visit. He was much moved by the spirit he experienced among us. He said many times that it reminded him very much of the times of Blumhardt in Bad Boll. "It is not like that among us any more now," he told us. Eberhard discussed two Blumhardt volumes with him at the time, *Das Reich Gottes* ("The Kingdom of God") and *Nachfolge Christi* ("The Following of Christ"). Both had been compiled by Eugen Jäckh and published by us.

Yes, the Blumhardts, father and son, and their expectation of God's Kingdom played an important part in our circles. The Kingdom of God, which already today is a powerful living force among us, giving us both enthusiasm and a form of life, was living among us then. We read about the healing of the sick and the driving out of demons at the time of the father Blumhardt with the innermost interest and concern, as we experienced similar things in our own midst again and again, when the Spirit worked among us in a particularly powerful

way. To tell about this is difficult. Perhaps I can say more later
about how such experiences shook and moved our whole circle.
Above all, our longing and hope was directed with great fervor
and zeal toward the Kingdom of the future when love and
justice will rule over the whole world, the whole cosmos. How
much did we love the song *Tochter Zion, freue dich!* ("Daughter of Zion, rejoice!") which we sang again and again, both
in summer and winter. Also "Lo, a light is in the East" and
*Es weht der Wind ein Rauschen her* ("Now blows the wind
and sighs dismay"), songs which were written in our own circle
and taken up and sung enthusiastically.

Leonhard Ragaz, who unfortunately never visited us, also
had much to say to us. He had just given up his professorship
and moved to the Gartenhofstrasse in Zurich because of the
love he felt for the working classes. His challenges and articles
in the magazine *Neue Wege* ("New Ways") spoke to us very
much. They were often read aloud in our inner meetings, and
gripped us and shook us up as a circle. This was especially the
case with his articles, "Following Christ" and "Faithfulness,"
which I still remember. Leonhard Ragaz was a particular
voice speaking to us at that time.

It was similar with Kees Boeke in Holland, who called men
to a life of action. During the post-war period Kees and his
wife Betty had started a Brotherhood House in Bilthoven. Betty
Boeke was a Cadbury, related to the Cadbury chocolate manu-
facturers in England, and therefore of some means. Kees and
Betty felt called to live in brotherhood and to give all their
possessions to the poor. I had met Kees during the winter of
1920–1921 when he, together with several delegates of the
Fellowship of Reconciliation, came to Sannerz to have talks
with us about the "new life." Others who took part were Oliver
Dryer from England, John Nevin Sayre from America and

Henri Rosier from France, and there may have been more. For all of us this had been the first meeting with representatives of the "enemy" countries. These talks with them were inexpressibly moving. Each one of these men wanted to help with the building up of a new world, a new age, in a new spirit, the spirit of reconciliation and brotherliness. This made us feel full of courage and hope for the future of God on earth!

Another important visit was that of the calligrapher Rudolf Koch, who was to become well-known throughout Germany. He spent some days with us. He also belonged to the men of the future and took an active part in the movements of the time. While he was staying with us the house was full to overflowing with guests, and it became necessary to write a kind of guest letter, something like a house rule. Rudolf Koch wrote this out in his bold, beautiful script, and we fixed the sheet to the wall of the dining room.

This was also the time when the following lines came to be written:

> Ten were invited, but twenty people came;
> Put water in the soup and welcome them all the same!

In this respect we were hardly lacking in generosity. Our kitchen was of the simplest kind imaginable. It sometimes happened that the cook (though in fact we did not have anyone who could properly be called a cook) was sitting outside in the open, doing a landscape painting or writing poetry, while the soup or the potatoes boiled over onto the fire. Naturally the wood fire was put out or the soup was burned. Nobody worried about it; we would just sing together good-humoredly,

> Cook, what's for supper tonight?
> Noodles, oh thunder and blight!
> Burned were they by the flame;

> Cook, is this not a shame?
> Noodles all burned so black,
> Fit neither for dog nor cat.

As I said earlier, we grown-ups did not care very much about these things, as we had not exactly been spoiled during the four years of war and revolution. I myself had very little time for cooking, on account of the many guests who came to us. Our young girls were either factory workers, typists and teachers, or they had come from well-to-do, pampered homes, like our cook during this period, Margarethe D. I found these conditions hard only on account of the children. Already at that time we had children among us who had come to us from conditions of great want. Some of them were very small, not more than one or two years old. People had simply brought them to us. There were some people who just could not understand that these children were in need of specially nourishing food. One person said, "Why should the children have milk or eggs, instead of eating herrings, beans and dried peas as we grown-ups do? Don't we want to share everything?"

Otto Salomon, Eva Öhlke, Suse Hungar and Gertrud Cordes were the members of our first circle, in addition to Eberhard, Else and myself. Here I want to tell about the wedding of Gertrud Cordes with the young medical doctor Hermann Thoböll. Gertrud was the daughter of a wealthy businessman. We were friends of the family and in the early years of our marriage had been their guests at their country residence at Fleestett near Hittfeld on a number of occasions. The wedding was to be celebrated completely in the style of the youth movement, as the bride and bridegroom wanted it to be. They did not want such "bourgeois" affairs as a church wedding, a bridal wreath of myrtle or a bridal veil. Eberhard and I, as well as Heinrich Schultheiss, were invited to the wedding. The

parents of both bride and bridegroom had everything prepared
for a very middle-class wedding, but the young couple refused
to wear the formal coat with tails, the white wedding gown,
and so on. Hermann Thoböll appeared in a grass-green tunic
and shorts, Gertrud in a simple white dress with a garland of
red clover blossoms in her hair. We walked behind the couple
with music and singing, through green meadows. There we sat
down in a circle in the grass. Even the "bourgeois" parents
sat down with us!

Eberhard was to conduct the wedding, in the manner of the
Quakers and of the youth movement. I no longer remember
what was read or spoken, but it had to do with love, faithfulness
in marriage, and the true Church. All this seemed very strange,
particularly to Father and Mother Thoböll. Afterwards Judge
Thoböll, Hermann's father, demanded an official Church certificate of the marriage. As I recall it now, Heinrich Schultheiss,
who had been a minister, wrote out the required certificate.
Faithfulness in monogamy was the strong witness at this
wedding.

To continue about our little group at Sannerz: At that time
the group was not close-knit and welded together in such a
way that one could speak of a group belonging together for
life. Among the guests the first circle was called "the holy
seven." We all wore the open ring of the early Church, which
was also worn by other friends of the movement. We were a
fighting band, in the process of growth. We talked everything
over together and fought everything through together.

Toward the end of the year 1921 the circle of those who
carried the responsibility of the life together had grown rapidly,
perhaps too rapidly. Of those who had been our guests and
helpers during the summer a considerable number, more than
forty, had stayed on to spend the winter with us. Because of

a dry summer and our urban background the harvest had been a poor one. However, the publishing work was doing well, and a lot of work was put into it. Otto Salomon worked there, Fritz Schloss, "Böhmchen" who came from the Furche Publishing House, Lotte Scriba, Hedwig Buxbaum, Eva Öhlke, but most of all Tata (Else) and Eberhard, who worked together particularly on the magazine *Das Neue Werk*. All told, it was quite a crew that worked in the three front rooms of the ground floor. Nearly every day somebody had to walk to the printer's in Schlüchtern, a distance of one and a half hours of walking. Quite a number of books were published in the course of these first years.

Eberhard had won an old friend from his earlier correspondence to help us with the farming. This friend came to us with his young wife. He was a very nice fellow, a true idealist, but he knew almost nothing about farming. First, he wanted to let the villagers remove the dung heap from the front yard free of charge, because it was such an eyesore! Naturally, the farmers in the village were horrified at such ignorance. He also fetched whole cartloads of bean poles from the forest with the proud comment, "We'll soon have it down, the wood of the Baroness von Stumm!" (She was the wealthy owner of the nearby castle at Ramholz.) Unfortunately he had forgotten to plant the beans! To the great amusement of the villagers he would sit under the cow, with his big, horn-rimmed glasses, milking and making verses at the same time. Well, all this did not exactly make for much confidence in our farming methods.

Our educational work went better. Suse Hungar was a trained teacher and so was Trudi Dalgas, now Hüssy, who joined us in October 1921. Trudi had been a young teacher at Frankfurt, and there she had heard Eberhard speak in the Adult Education Center (*Volksschulheim*) in the spring. She came to our Whitsun Conference and gave up her job to come and work with us, full of energy and joy for the cause that filled us. Moni, my sister, arrived the same day. She had given up her job as a midwife in Halle, at the beginning quite simply because after visiting us during the summer, she liked our way of life.

My eldest sister Olga and her adopted daughter Ruth, who was seven years old at the time, had also been staying with us during this summer (1921). She was in need of a rest because of her lung illness, and derived benefit from the good fresh air of the Rhön. Our life had made a great impression on her, but as our house was full to overflowing at the time, we advised her to accept the invitation for several months of a Javanese princess, Maria Moijen, who was running a home in Holland for the benefit of women, particularly mothers, who were victims of the serious malnutrition resulting from the war years. To our distress, a year later we had to fetch her from a village in Lippe in a very serious condition. She had then been staying in the home of a friendly teacher there.

Yes, all sorts of people had come to stay with us at the beginning of that fall and winter! To begin with, we realized we would be unable to support this increased number, about sixty all told, through the winter and that we would have to find some source of income at least for that time. We thought of basket-making or needlework, for instance making the Schlitz style of house-shoes or slippers, or something like that. When we considered this question together, the differences in outlook became apparent. The question was asked, for example, whether we were really in a position to accept so many children into our household, as long as we were not able to support our own children. Actually, we had not fetched the children; they had simply been brought to our house!

During this time a second family joined us with their two

little girls—Heinrich S., a very radical parson from Gelnhaar in the Vogelsberg Mountains, and his wife Elisabeth. As a result of his views, he could not continue as a parson; hence he came to stay with us. His wife was very middle-class in outlook and wanted to continue living her accustomed life in our midst. Soon tensions arose between the two, husband and wife. However, it did go fairly well until after Christmas. All were still able to take their parts in the play, "The Child of God," which we rehearsed together with much feeling.

Otto Salomon, with his songs and poems, gave special expression to what was moving among us all in the whole household. The day before Christmas all of us boarded a truck belonging to our friend Wolf, a soap manufacturer. Already dressed up for the Christmas play we drove to Schlüchtern to play for the workers in the employ of Victor Wolf.

After Christmas we concerned ourselves very much with Paul's Letter to the Romans, most of all with its eighth chapter, on the victory of the Spirit! It was in this context that, for the first time, one of our original circle of seven basically contradicted our direction. "How can we testify to Romans 8 if we still live in accordance with Romans 7?" he asked. He referred to Paul's words, "I do not do what I want, but I do the very thing I hate . . . . Who will deliver me from this body of death?" The answer then was given, that immediately after these words Paul says, "Thanks be to God through Jesus Christ our Lord!" and then, in the eighth chapter, "For the law of the Spirit of life in Christ Jesus has set me free from the law of sin and death." It is not that *we* have it. But we *can* have it. For the first time we felt he was not in the same faith: that the Spirit *can* rule everything and bring everything to us.

Many talks with him followed, personal ones and with the circle of the whole household. A year and a half before, when he joined the community, he had said, "I am the camel. You can put on my back anything that is too much for you." This beginning faith and humility was in contradiction to what he now felt. "If I were to surrender completely to the call, I would not be able to produce art." And, "Because you accept so many 'worthless' people into your midst, those who have some 'worth' are staying away more and more." Well, this did not sound like the first beginning anymore! No wonder, then, that one day he came to tell us that he had joined Georg Flemmig's Young Men's Fellowship, and that therefore he wanted to leave the growing Church-community.

This was a great shock and a great pain to us all. The first one to leave our ranks! He promised to remain in close contact with the brotherhood and to serve as a link, since there were many critical, even hostile voices making themselves heard already at that time. This can be seen in an article, "On Criticism of Sannerz," in *Das Neue Werk* of 1922. After his departure in January 1922, other voices came up within the communal household. In spite of this, we were led together again and again by the good Spirit.

> Arise and build up Zion,
> A glad and joyous Kingdom
> Where Jesus Christ is Lord!
> It must become much greater,
> That in the walls may gather
> All men that are upon the earth.
>
> Arise and build up Zion,
> A glad and joyous Kingdom,
> The City of our God!
> If we but work unwearied
> It soon will stand completed.
> O happy those who helped to build!

# CRISIS

IN OUR MOVEMENT of a new beginning, so full of promise, another influence soon made itself felt and heard, also in print. In particular it came from ministers of the various Churches. Their catchword was, "People with the new vision should now turn back to the old conditions of life, to be a small light there." Through this the impetus of the movement came to a halt for many of the young people.

The Whitsun Conference of 1922 took place not in Sannerz but in Wallroth, in the Rhön hills. The new "back to the old" movement had invited speakers, such as Wilhelm Stählin. The topics in themselves were an indication of the direction. "Fever and Salvation in the Youth Movement," "Sannerz (phantasy, Utopia) versus Habertshof (reality)." The Habertshof had accepted the new direction under the leadership of Emil Blum, a former Swiss pastor, of taking the new vision back to the old life.

Eberhard also spoke. Among other things, he spoke about the "funeral" of the New Work movement, and this gave great offense at the time. After this conference we continued to have many guests, including those who had been there, and there were many long evening discussions about the two directions of our movement in the circle of the household; people took their stand on one side or the other. The fight, then, had started within our own ranks! During all of this the work continued, in the publishing, in the office and on the farm, though certainly interrupted by exciting talks.

For the month of July 1922 our whole family was invited to Bilthoven in Holland. Already in the spring, Kees Boeke had given us money for the purchase of a mill, as Sannerz had become too small to house the increasing number of people. It was not worth our while to build more rooms in a house which, after all, was only rented. Some fine meadows and good fields belonged to this mill, which was situated in quite a romantic spot. The farmers in Sannerz had up to now rented us their poorest and stoniest fields, one reason being that we were so many people and therefore well able to gather the stones. They also felt that we just were not farmers, while they were in need of the best pieces of land for themselves. The fields that belonged to the mill were much better and so were a great attraction for us, especially as the publishing work could not support all sixty of us at that time. Also, to live and work with nature, the experience of sowing and harvesting, belonged to our new life.

As I mentioned before, our family was invited to spend the month of July in Bilthoven. Because we were rather run down in health after the years of malnutrition during the war and the two beginning years in Sannerz, the whole community decided that we should accept this invitation. Even though there was already much unrest in the community at the time, we agreed to the trip, trusting in the good Spirit to overcome all difficulties and differences, as He had done again and again. We also trusted in those who had fought through and suffered so many things with us, with great enthusiasm and in the joyful expectancy of the new Kingdom which Christ himself will establish. This was living in us very strongly; we did not think it was something far away, either!

We were welcomed in Holland and looked after there with great love. There was a lively, anti-militaristic spirit which thrived in that brotherhood group, so much under the strong spiritual influence of Kees and Betty Boeke. Every Saturday, as many as possible marched in front of the Town Hall in Amsterdam, singing Kees Boeke's song, "No, no, we have done with fighting," in various languages. Holland had been drawn into the war spirit of 1914 quite strongly. On the eighth anniversary of the outbreak of war, on August 2, 1922, a big crowd of those belonging to Bilthoven, together with other war resisters, marched through Amsterdam, with stuffed horses and peace flags with the inscription, "No More War." We also took part, of course, singing along with the others, "Long, long enough have Christian men borne arms and killed each other," together with other songs by Kees Boeke, all of these in Dutch. When the military columns marched past the Brotherhood House in Bilthoven, everyone opened the windows and shouted, *Nooit meer oorlog!* ("No more war!")

Kees and Betty Boeke had the same kind of attitude with regard to money. They never even touched money. When they passed through customs or crossed a toll bridge, they would give some eggs or something else instead of money. Neither did they pay any taxes, and on account of this they were put into prison again and again. At that time they also believed they should not obey the police. On one occasion Kees just lay flat on the ground and was carried off bodily. Their furniture and other possessions went up for auction over and over again, but soon their friends and wealthy relatives had refurnished their home (they had children too!) until the things were taken away from them again—and again.

In other respects, too, the circle was very "radical." Every guest or helper was able to take part in their meetings among themselves and *every* voice was of equal value. As Kees expressed it, every man carries a light within him and can speak from and be moved by the good Spirit. In the same way, everyone was allowed to speak to the practical questions which arose. We took part in such brotherhood meetings on a number of occasions and it seemed rather chaotic to us. What we missed, and this we also expressed, was the Church of Christ, where such freedom would be possible; the Spirit in which every voice can speak.

In any case, Kees and Betty impressed us as very genuine; they were people who carried their recognitions into action. Thus we were able to accept and learn a number of things from them.

During this time we received letters from home concerning the situation there, which sounded quite disquieting. For one thing, the financial situation was very hard, as the inflation was growing from day to day and money became more and more worthless. The currency was going into millions and billions. As a result of this, moneys which were given to the publishing work as an investment by friends, and in one case also by a cooperative bank, were called in, and we were expected to make payment within a few days. Eberhard was asked to return home. As it was impossible to raise money in Germany, we regarded it as providential that we happened to be in Holland, and we felt inwardly confident that what was needed would be given to us there. Thus Eberhard wrote to the community that he would be back before payment was due, that is, in two weeks at the utmost.

In spite of this the unrest at home increased more and more. This we were able to feel across the distance and also through the letters that came. During a long walk across the heath, Eberhard received the inner certainty that he should not allow himself to be jerked out of his inner calm, but should complete his tasks in Holland as previously arranged, to be home again in time for the date when payment on the loan became due. As I was ready to travel with the children I was surprised at first that Eberhard wanted to stay, because I was very much aware of the unrest at home. We considered the situation together with Else, who had accompanied us as secretary, and arrived at the same conclusion together with Eberhard. We felt a deep and strong inner assurance that God would show us the way and would help us. In the meantime, letters arrived speaking of a gross lack of responsibility.

Here I want to quote from a letter written by Eberhard to Trudi Dalgas (now Hüssy) in July of 1922.

> Take courage! We must no longer see what is small! The great must take hold of us in such a way that it also penetrates and transforms the small. I have courage and joy for our life again in the certainty, of course, that it will cost a great and glorious struggle. The Spirit will conquer the flesh! The Spirit is the stronger! He overwhelms me, you, one after the other. This Spirit is goodness, independence, mobility.

> Our life will become not narrower, but broader; not more limited, but more boundless; not more regulated, but more abundant; not more pedantic, but more bounteous; not more sober, but more enthusiastic; not more faint-hearted, but more daring; not worse and more human, but filled with God and ever better; not sadder, but happier; not more incapable, but more creative. All this is Jesus and His Spirit of freedom! He is coming to us. Therefore let us not grieve about anything, but forgive everyone, just as we must be forgiven everything, and go into the future radiant with joy. Stay and wait until you are clothed with power from on high.

Those who were in charge at Sannerz during our short leave of absence had written to the leaders of the Bilthoven Brotherhood House that they should send whatever money they wanted to give Sannerz, to the home address, rather than give it to us. The Bilthoven Brotherhood House did not heed this advice. Our departure came quickly. We left in the beginning of August and spent a brief night in Frankfurt. On the farewell evening a lady handed us an envelope containing Dutch guilders. When Eberhard went to the bank in the morning he received in German money exactly the amount that was due on that date; for in this case the devaluation or inflation had worked to our advantage. Although Eberhard informed the people at home of this by telephone, the answer was, "It is too late now; the publishing house is already in liquidation!"

We traveled home after this. Suse Hungar met us at the station in Schlüchtern. She looked almost petrified and said only that she was not to tell us anything. At home we had an icy-cold reception, and watery soup. A small cake had been baked for the children, however.

We were invited to a meeting after supper. Everyone in the household was sitting in a circle on the floor of the dining hall, the largest room. The windows were wide open. A student conference was meeting in Schlüchtern at the time, and Eberhard was to give one of the main talks. Since the conference was taking place just in this town mainly to enable the participants to get to know Sannerz, it was only natural that many of the young people came over to experience something of the community in Sannerz. They sat on the windowsills or stood outside close to the windows while the following struggle was going on inside. Above all, it was said that we should change our whole direction. No longer: "Get out of the old conditions!" but rather: "Go right into them!" The people with new eyes must go right back into the old bourgeois life. Further, we were told that faith and economic matters never belong together, whereas we had represented that faith should penetrate and master everything, including financial matters. "The transcendent must enter the immanent."

Finally, it was said that the "open door" was nothing but a great lie, that we also had held meetings of both an inner and practical nature at which not everybody was present. These meetings we held mostly during the night, when everybody was in bed; we discussed the situation of the various guests and the atmosphere they brought with them, as we had to find a new way with them again and again! We also had meetings in which we gathered strength for the next stretch of the way ahead.

Well—this was not an easy beginning. Neither were the discussions that followed. An extremely dark atmosphere, mixed with hostility, was filling the room. When Eberhard stated that we did not want to change the direction and that we were willing to continue living with them in a modest, unassuming way if others would take over the leadership, the upheaval knew no bounds. One after the other stood up and declared that he would leave the community. There must have been about forty in all. We could hardly grasp all this, as with a good many of them we had had powerful inner experiences. What had happened during our absence of four weeks? It was just inconceivable to us.

At the end, when the one who was in charge of the meeting put the question as to who, after all, was going to stay, there were just seven, the smallest possible number to enable the "society" (the legal body of the group) to continue. Had there been fewer, for instance only six, the society would have been automatically dissolved, and the money for the mill, as well as all the inventory, would have been distributed among those who just happened to be living in the house.

Our business manager at the time was Kurt H., a former bank clerk. He also wanted to leave. Apart from him, the executive council consisted of Heinrich S. (who also wanted to leave us again with his family), as well as Eberhard and myself. Because two signatures were the minimum required for the transaction of business, everything could be done without Eberhard and myself. Our cows and all the other chattels were sold off. The reason given was that it was not possible for city people to look after them properly. Glass jars were bought to enable all those moving away to take as much as possible of the plentiful fruit and vegetables along with them. The firewood we had stacked up for the winter was burned in the stoves in September—with the windows wide open. Even the money for the mill was used, for purchasing overcoats, shirts and other clothes. We were asked to do likewise. The rage exceeded all bounds when we refused to accept any share of the money given for the mill, needed as it was for the economic basis of the community. Words like fraud, swindle, big lies, etc. were hurled at us from all sides. Obviously the situation was becoming quite impossible.

However, those who were leaving had first to find a livelihood elsewhere. In the beginning the Heinrich S. family were looking for another possibility for community living, together with several others. After a while they found this in Gelnhausen, not far from us, in a former children's home there. No wonder that this community only survived for a few months, as there was nothing to hold it together except the protest against *our* way.

The weeks and months we were still together were almost unbearable, no doubt for all who were concerned. Among those we had with us, there were several girls who had been under the care of public welfare. They had not come to us from an inner urge. One of them had been entrusted to our care by the welfare office; the other had come to be delivered of her illegitimate child. Both attempted to spread this or that bad rumor from one to another in the house, which did not make life any easier at all.

Our little circle had undertaken to do the cooking for the whole household. I did most of it, but as I was not used to the thin, green, watery soups, I tried to cook better food, though in smaller quantities. The others felt that we wanted to starve them. Eberhard immediately asked me to increase the quantities. We made it clear to ourselves that this was the hour to act in accordance with the words of Jesus in the Sermon on the Mount. Thus I started cooking again directly after each meal. Some of the others gathered mushrooms or picked fruit to make jam or to preserve in glass jars.

This situation—having no community but living together in the same house—became more and more intolerable as the days went on. Help came to us through the visit of Ernst Ferdinand Klein, the same uncle who had invited Eberhard to his parsonage in Lichtenrade near Berlin in 1899 and who had helped Eberhard toward his conversion. He had come to us from Berlin with his wife Lisbeth to experience the spirit of Sannerz. But what did he find? At first this uncle did not take sides, but in his loving way tried to bring about a reconciliation. When he was not successful in this, as far as the opposition was concerned, he knocked at every door throughout the whole house every morning, inviting everybody to come to a devotional meeting! Nobody was able to resist this loving man; everybody came, and this often helped to make the situation more bearable. Although there were very lovable people among those who were leaving, people who had been very moved at one time, now a spirit of hatred was demonstrated by all of them. This was simply because we were determined to continue on the way we had seen and because we did not consider this way as an experiment in living as the others did, an experiment for which, it was said, "our generation is just too weak, too human, too selfish."

Here I want to mention the liquidation of the Neuwerk Publishing House. The partners or shareholders met officially to wind up the publishing work, which had not been run in a business-like way, in their opinion. The published books were divided up because those who were leaving us were planning to start a publishing house of their own, and intended to take over some of the most suitable books for this, such as *Junge Saat* ("Young Seed"), both Blumhardt volumes, the books by Georg Flemmig, as well as others, but above all the magazine *Das Neue Werk*. It was an act of friendship on the part of Otto H., who died soon afterwards, to leave the Zinzendorf volume with us. He said, "We respect Eberhard's faith, even though we cannot share it." He was of the opinion that spiritual and temporal matters should not be mixed together.

At the end of the meeting the question was asked whether all were in agreement with the liquidation. There was a unanimous "Yes"—except for Eberhard, who got up to say, "With the exception of one voice! I am not in agreement. Please record this in the minutes!"

In October at last the house became empty. Yet there was still a great obstacle to overcome. Those who were leaving had gone to the lodgings office, a government office, declaring that the house was going to be empty and that rooms would be available for people who were in need of a place to live, of whom there were many after the war. Consequently we were summoned to appear before the local court in Schlüchtern.

The judge was in possession of a plan of the whole house which showed the arrangement of the rooms. They had the keenest and most severe attorney on their side, while Eberhard and I were quite alone. We made it clear that the work of the community had not been closed down, nor had its social work been discontinued. Both would be going on, only a number of people were leaving.

This was not an easy day for us, as the lawyer for the plaintiffs put forward their case in a most energetic way. Although we were aware of the situation and of the lawyer's reputation, Eberhard and I had walked down to Schlüchtern full of courage and confidence in a good outcome. We mentioned that very close to us, in Ramholz, the castle of the families von Stumm and von Kühlmann was standing empty almost the whole year round. So we put forward our point of view strongly. Solemnly the judge gave the decision that the court had recognized that the law was on our side and that, as a result, we would be permitted to continue with the use of the Sannerz house for our needs and for the objects and purposes of our work. Naturally, when we came home again there was great rejoicing. Now we just had to continue building up with energy, after the departure of so many beloved people who had stood with us in the original enthusiasm for the new way on which we had started.

In spite of all these sad experiences and disillusionments it was not the case that the "worse" ones had left and that the "better" or "stronger" ones had stayed on. This we did not feel at all. We were very much aware of our own mistakes and weaknesses and knew that we simply were not adequate for the real thing! Yet in spite of our inability we felt a strong urge to dare to go on, in spite of ourselves. The following was written by me later and published in *The Plough*, introducing

Eberhard's own words about this time of crisis:

In 1922 there were many changes. Many of our friends turned back to the old life. They were disillusioned: they said that people today were too individualistic to be able to give themselves up to the extent of being capable of community living. We felt the same incapability in ourselves, but we had heard the challenge of community life so distinctly that, for all our apprehension, we were determined to go through with it. Only seven ventured to begin again; all the rest went away. Objectively, the chief reason for the separation was the issue of faith versus purely economic considerations. In a talk with some of our guests later on, Eberhard said of this time of crisis and new beginning:

"When the call first came to us, we felt that the Spirit of Jesus Christ had urged us and charged us to live in full community, in communal solidarity, with an open door and a loving heart for all people. It was the Word of Jesus Christ, the reality of His life and the fact of His Spirit, that gave us the strength to start firmly and certainly on this way and to keep on though our steps were short and feeble. When we had traveled only a short way on this path, times came upon us that put this power to the test, hostile times of trial, when friends we knew well and whom we had grown to love deeply, suddenly reversed their position and became enemies of the way, because they had turned away from freedom and unity, because they wanted to go back again into ordinary middle-class life, to normal private life and their own pocketbook. At the time, the movement was led into bondage again through the middle-class influences of capitalism and its business and professional life.

"But though most of our friends left us, though whole groups had deserted the flag of unity and freedom, though well-meaning friends might earnestly advise us that the way of freedom and unity would lead us to a lonely and ineffectual end, that could not change anything. With our own children and those we had adopted, we had to push through toward the goal."[1]

Eberhard and Else, who had gone to Berlin for a publishing talk, brought back with them a ten-year-old boy, Hans Grimm, a motherless child from the most difficult family circumstances. During these same days we received a telegram from a teacher in the Detmold district, telling us that our sister Olga, then forty years old, was asking us to fetch her. She had fallen ill with tuberculosis a year and a half earlier and had stayed with us, together with her adopted daughter Ruth, eight years old at the time, during the summer of 1921. Now it seemed that she was in the last stages of her illness.

Moni and I traveled to Olga immediately and really found her sick unto death. Both of us were very much moved and impressed by her attitude of faith. She told us how hard it had been for her and what a struggle she had been through when she had realized that she had little time left to live, but that she had fought it through and that she now was full of joyful anticipation of eternity, of the "City of golden lanes," of Jesus, also of Paul and John, also of her parents and brothers and sister who had gone ahead. She was full of regret, too — it was the beginning of November — that she would never experience spring again, the earthly spring with its violets, wild cowslips and other flowers; but she was looking forward eagerly to the Eternal Spring! Especially on our journey home we spoke only of eternal things. We had rented a special railroad coach,

[1] *The Plough,* Autumn 1953, pp. 6–7.

which was coupled to various trains en route, so that Olga did not have to change trains, which she would have been unable to do in her condition. Little Ruth traveled with us in the same coach. She was nine years old at the time, and was to live with us henceforth as part of our family.

These last few weeks we were able to experience with Olga were a great challenge to all of us. So close to death! But also to the life which lasts eternally. It was a symbol of what we went through during the preceding months and were still experiencing then. Death and resurrection. The senior minister of Schlüchtern, Mr. Orth, who visited Olga during her last days, said, "For her, passing into the other world is like going from one room to the other."

The outward circumstances of nursing her were not easy. Moni had taken on the main task of nursing, and I took turns with her during certain hours to give her a chance for sleeping and walking in the fresh air. We would have liked Olga to stay at the hospital in Schlüchtern because of the better conditions there, but she asked us very much to be allowed to die at home with her sisters, in the small circle of believers.

We were able to put at her disposal a good, relatively large room, with two big windows facing south. But the question of heating! We had not had the money to buy firewood again and had scarcely any coal. We only had the branches we were allowed to gather in the woods of the Albing Mountain, which too often were green and wet. Every day as many of us as possible went into the woods to collect firewood for all the stoves that had to be heated, and there were many of these. In particular our boys, between the ages of seven and ten, had to help vigorously in this job. They enjoyed doing this; like all the work, it was done with eagerness and enthusiasm. But the situation with footwear was just catastrophic!

Well, in Olga's room also, there stood one of these small iron stoves. It was smoking all the time on account of the wood which was nearly always wet and green. Because of this Olga had very bad attacks of coughing and found it very hard to breathe. This often was terrible to watch. Nevertheless, there was a wonderful atmosphere in the room. Eternity was very close to all of us. Often we sat at her bedside in small groups, Else, Moni, Trudi, Hugga (Suse Hungar) and Eberhard and I. We sang a great many of our old and new Advent songs. Often one was alone with the dying Olga, listening to her longing for redemption from suffering and her expectation of glory. Little Ruth was allowed to visit her only once every day, because of the danger of infection. Olga encouraged her in her own childlike way, expressing the hope she felt for her that one day she would find the right way to Christ.

On her last night, the night of December 1, shortly before the first Sunday of Advent, I was sent to bed because I had flu with a fever. We did not know that this would be her last night. Ruth and Emi-Ma were in the room next to mine, Olga in the room directly above. Suddenly I heard a loud voice calling from the adjoining room, and both girls came rushing into my room. While I was still talking with the children, which lasted for about half an hour, I heard the door being locked above me. I knew, even before my sisters could tell me, that Olga had died.

Eberhard was in Sonnefeld at the time, meeting with a circle of moved young Baptists, the circle of Hans Klassen, out of which the settlement of the Neu-Sonnefeld Youth was to come into being later. Thus he had not been with us for a few days. A telegram brought him home quickly, so that he was able to celebrate the First of Advent, December 3, with us. The Advent songs fitted our experience perfectly, especially

the song, "How shall I fitly meet Thee?" We sang all the
verses with the innermost movement of the heart, while the
body of our dear Olga lay in her little room. We also sang
Otto Salomon's song, "Lo, a light is in the East" and many
other songs.

The following day we had the funeral in Ramholz. The
coffin was taken to the Ramholz cemetery by way of Vollmerz
on a simply decorated farm wagon.

This death, or rather, this going home to Christ, had no
terror for us. We felt so strongly that death already held within
it the power of resurrection. It reminded us sharply of the
experiences of 1922—death and resurrection. None of us will
ever forget the meaning of this experience as long as we live
on this earth. During this first crisis we had felt strongly the
powers of death at work in the movement which had been
awakened to life, and we had become very much aware of
the weakness and the needs of our own persons. Yet out of
this very crisis, like a breath of spring, new hope and new
strength had arisen for the cause for which we wanted to
fight at all costs.

Nevertheless, a hard struggle lay ahead, and we had to
remind ourselves again and again of this experience.

# A NEW START

WE WOULD HAVE LIKED to be among ourselves for a time. However, we did not remain alone. Many curious people came who wanted to know how things were getting on in Sannerz; often there were criticisms. Expressions like, "Sannerz is just one big lie" or "Sannerz is nothing but a utopia," had stuck in the memories of many. We could not disprove anything with words; the only way to do this was through the life as a whole.

Friedel, the welfare girl, returned to us expecting a baby. She had already been received into our household in Berlin, as a helper, and we had taken her in again in 1920 after she had been caught stealing in a big department store when on leave from us; she had served her term in prison. She had left us during the months of crisis in the summer.

We are often asked what our attitude to social work was in those early years. This was not a problem for us, since we took in all those who came to us asking for help. During the years after the war, too, many people whose lives were broken came to us. Among these were several expectant mothers who had heard about us somehow and were in real need. This caused serious offense to the people in the district where we lived, which was Catholic, and it did not improve our reputation. Moni was a trained midwife and therefore able to do this work, and we all supported her. To us all, this was a deed of love and assistance.

As regards fruits of these efforts, there were practically nothing but disappointments! The mothers disappeared soon, with or without baby, after having regained strength among us, gratis of course! Was this to stop us from doing the work of love? This question came up, naturally, especially because of the loss of our reputation. We, however, rejected this temptation again and again as cowardice. Although there was little thankfulness for this work, it was not for the sake of thanks that we did it.

Karl, called Roland, came with a group of boys, just in time to help us to get the last potatoes out of the ground. They also helped us to gather firewood from the forest. Just at Christmas time, Agnes W., with a small group of girls, came for a visit. We had a feeling that we were being observed, rather than that our guests wanted to experience something with us. Often this was not easy. Yet, even during this period, we did find time and occasion for quiet inner gathering. Eberhard's song, "Twilight deepening, hope disappearing" expressed what all of us were feeling. A little time later our experiences found a special expression in the poem, *Ich fange wieder an zu leben* ("I start again anew to live"). Walther Böhme wrote the tunes for both these songs.

Our house remained open, children were brought to us, people came visiting again—the curious as well as the seeking. However, everything went at a much slower pace, and we found more time and quiet to build up the children's community, so important to us from the beginning. The older children, Emi-Margret, Hardi and Heini, had not remained unaffected by the great turmoil of 1922. They too were aware of that spirit which can be called hatred; they had heard such remarks as, "Sannerz is just a big lie. It should be destroyed lock, stock and barrel." Eberhard had been badly abused and defamed. It was really a great miracle that we were able to continue in spite of it all. We attended conferences, mostly two of us together, and it was noticeable how many people would move away from us when they heard that we had come from Sannerz.

The publishing house also was to get on its feet again. It was now called the Eberhard Arnold Publishing House, because those who had left wanted to keep the name Neuwerk, as this name was already known. As far as books were concerned, we kept only Otto Herpel's *Zinzendorf*, two dramas which Otto Salomon had brought with him, the book on the race problem by Goldstein and the little volume of legends. Tolstoi's *Religious Letters* and Emil Engelhardt's book on love and marriage were just being printed at the time.

Because Kees Boeke had left to us the remaining part of the money given for the mill we had at least a little money to continue our work, after all deductions for the group that had left were made. Through our connections with the Baptist Youth we took over with them the magazine *Die Wegwarte*.[1] A new relationship developed with the Hochweg Publishing House in Berlin. Eberhard's idea of a library of source material could be realized in this way.

It meant a great enrichment for us all to be able to share in the witness of other periods and movements when these volumes of source material came into being. When we sorted potatoes in the spring or did other appropriate work, such as stirring jam in the basement, the proof sheets would be read aloud to us, and really everybody took a lively interest in this. For instance, when *The Early Christians* was being written, a book which Eberhard himself compiled, we were able to participate in selecting significant and suitable passages from the material which was read aloud to us all.

[1] The wildflower, chicory. *Wegwarte* means one who waits or helps on the way.

The authors of several of the books that were being written at that time came to visit us, to make it possible for us to share in their work. They were Alexander Beyer, author of the volume on Francis of Assisi; Karl Justus Obenauer, author of *Novalis*; Hermann Ulrich, who edited the Diaries of Kierkegaard; and Alfred Wiesenhuetter, editor of *Jakob Böhme*. In this way we were led to an understanding of the historical context of these books.

Because I had been interested from my early youth in religious songs and hymns and also had selected most of the songs that we sang together, I was asked to make a selection of Zinzendorf's songs in their original form from the Moravian archives in Herrnhut. They were to be appended to Otto Herpel's volume on Zinzendorf. This work I enjoyed doing very much, and at appropriate opportunities I also read aloud those songs that seemed particularly suitable to me. Two books on which we were especially keen in those days were never finished. They were Eberhard's Anabaptist book (on the non-resistant Anabaptists of the sixteenth century) and Professor Theo Spira's volume on George Fox.

We worked on the book *Sonnenlieder* ("Songs of the Sun") with great enthusiasm. It meant a great deal of joy to us, but also a lot of work. Our trips to the printer Stürtz in the old, romantic town of Würzburg were most memorable and enjoyable. While Eberhard and Else went to the printer's, I did some shopping. The hours of proofreading we spent together in the Café Zeissner were just wonderful!

Life went on in the meantime. The school and the educational work were growing. How glorious were our trips in the summer when we went picking blueberries! We would stay away from home with the children for days on end to gather in the harvest given by God. At the same time we frequently would have rehearsed a play, a fairy tale play for instance, such as "The Water of Life," which we and the children produced under the old village linden tree of Altengronau. Or we would sing the old folk songs, accompanied by violins and guitars, and the peasants would treat us to bread, sausage and eggs in return! Our wagon would come out after a few days to carry home our harvest of berries, "which God had given us without our sowing," as Eberhard always said. And this harvest, often amounting to over 100 lbs., was definitely worthwhile! The joy, in which the children especially shared; the sense of fellowship; the experience of spending the whole day in the forest and spending the nights sleeping in a barn; the friendships which were made with the peasants of the neighborhood; the playing and singing together—all this meant great and deep joy.

In general we all had much more time with the children now, fifteen or more of them, including our own five. It was in those years that the "Sun Troop" came into being. The first one was begun by Heini, Sophie and Luise. These three felt a particularly strong urge to carry their inner experiences, their faith in Christ, their sense of fellowship, to the other children in the village. It was not easy, at times, to hold them back until they became older and more mature, when their urge simply to go out was such a strong one. These children were about ten, eleven and twelve years old at the time. Eberhard certainly had the greatest understanding of this childlike enthusiasm which made them place the things that filled their hearts above their homework or the small duties or chores. I was reminded very strongly of the Children's Crusades, and the children's revival at the time of Zinzendorf.

Nearly all the children of this age group joined the Sun Troop. They had a red banner. With this banner flying they would walk to a quiet meadow or to a place in the woods to hold their children's meeting. They would talk things over together, sing together or read from the Bible, or a legend, or from Meister Eckhart, I believe, whom Heini loved particularly. They had their own fires and their own songs. They did not like it if there was any eavesdropping, but would invite one or the other to share in their meeting. The following song was written during this time, in which Heini put into words what they experienced in their own childlike way:

> We would a fire kindle,
> Eagerly with great joy;
> We would a song be singing,
> That makes our hearts rejoice.
> Fire toward Christ shall blazing start,
> To all shall bring a new loving heart,
> Shall brightly shine afar.

Emi-Ma's song of 1922, which she wrote before the great crisis, was also much loved by them and they sang it often:

> When our brothers prepare for battle
> And in their breasts a fire is kindled,
> They march through town and countryside
> With courage and victorious cries.

> They wander with an impulse holy
> To sow the seeds of love to brothers.
> They fight against all war and strife,
> They fight against all sinfulness.

> They march with truly joyful hearts,
> With truly clear and bright sun-hearts,
> And Jesus Christ before them goes,
> And after Him run all who can.

The tune for this poem was composed by Marcel Woitzschach at the time when the struggles were beginning in 1922. He felt very much drawn by life in brotherhood, but also felt quite disillusioned by it. He was carried off with the experience of 1922. He was a coffee-house musician, and we never heard of him since, unfortunately.

Several years later a second Sun Troop was formed. In this our Monika, Rudi, Wolfgang and Gertrud were the leading elements, while Gerd and Liesel also took an active part. This group came into being in 1928 in just the same genuine way as the other one, yet it was somewhat different from the first one. I remember how this Sun Troop would meet almost daily during the year 1930, when Eberhard was in America. Monika, who was twelve years old at the time, had to stay in bed for a prolonged period because she had pleurisy with fever, which was diagnosed only later. During this time the Sun Troop would meet at her bedside. Because of the struggles and talks they were having among themselves her temperature went up to 104 degrees every evening, so that ultimately I had to stop these meetings! To make up for this, Monika asked me to have a little meeting with the children every afternoon until the time when she should be well again. We did this together, walking up to the meadow in the woods where the burial ground now is. I usually read to them a little legend or something else suitable, and we talked together. However, when they wanted to get clear about something or take other children into their group, they wished to be among themselves and I then left them alone.

During this time the work of the school was going ahead well. Apart from Trudi, our old Suse Hungar was working there. Ludwig Wedel also came to help out for a while. He was very much impressed by Eastern mysticism. After he left us he went to India, where he lived in an ashram for a number of years. Anneliese Dietrich, who came from the circle of Lene Thimme in Bremen, also helped us in the school for a few years.

In 1923 Georg Barth visited us for the first time. He helped with the boys in teaching handicrafts and practical work. He was a trained arts and crafts teacher and had worked for a time in a home for difficult boys. He belonged to the mystics of the contemporary youth movement, and his visit meant an enrichment for our circle, small as it was at the time. He was close to the Köngen Youth circle, which was under the strong influence of Wilhelm Hauer, who had given an address at our Whitsun Conference of 1921. Georg came back in 1925 to stay with us.

The year 1924 brought a special event. A family joined us for the first time since 1922. Adolf Braun,[2] who had been among us several times before, taking part in small conferences, decided to join, together with his wife Martha and their two little girls, Gertrud, four years old, and Elfriede, six months old. As they were on their way to us, in the railroad station of Kassel, "friends" from the year 1922 tried to persuade them against this step. However, they did come, in full trust. When he was in the army during World War I, Adolf had read the first edition of *Innenland*, and this had drawn his attention to us for the first time. He had sold his small house in Nordhausen and they arrived with a huge van full of furniture. They were completely ready to live with us in the plainest simplicity and poverty, particularly Adolf, who knew us from his previous visits.

We went to meet them, full of joyful anticipation, with a farm wagon decorated with greenery and flowers, the young people and children carrying torches. This was a very special

[2] Adolf Braun died in Primavera, Paraguay, in October 1948.

day for all of us. Here was another family, determined to make this venture together with their children! Our enthusiasm was great. Others who came from the same circle were Rose, now Kaiser, and, a few weeks later, Lottchen.

Adolf found his feet among us rather well. Our poverty he did not find difficult. He wanted only to keep the minimum of the furniture they brought. In his opinion, a few simple chairs, with a box to serve as a table, were ample. Martha was a little more "bourgeois" at first. We wanted the very simplest and plainest for everything. This was the tendency in the youth movement at the time.

During very difficult financial crises in times to come, Adolf was often the one who would go ahead, full of courage, extending the due dates of bills and notes and arranging for postponement of payments. This often meant that he had to be away for several days and nights at a time. He often was a great help, and he soon was elected to the executive council of the legal society. Eberhard and I, as well as Trudi and Adolf, were members of this council. Else (Tata) and Eberhard were the executives of the Eberhard Arnold Publishing House. The five of us enjoyed going to Schlüchtern together—in later times to Fulda—when we had to sign papers or to make purchases. (Fulda was the place from 1926 on, after we had bought the largest farm of the Sparhof for the Rhön Bruderhof during that year.) We always spent some very pleasant hours in the Café Hesse or in the cheap Ballmeyer Restaurant, near the Beate candle store in Fulda. Unforgettable hours these, often immediately after we had been concerning ourselves with some very difficult financial questions.

During the years after 1922 we also experienced some particularly hard struggles with demonic powers. These powers had been strongly provoked by the war and the revolution.

Thus several very tormented people came to us during this time, whose struggle for the good, Holy Spirit became ever stronger and came to a climax, the more powerfully the Spirit was at work in our midst. With some, a freeing from these powers was given in a more quiet way. There were two people in particular, however, who were tormented and enslaved by unclean and evil spirits, where I and others took part in the fight against these powers in a special way. Times like these cannot be forgotten by any one of us. Here we were concerned not only with flesh and blood; here we became involved in the spirit of the atmospheres, in the fight of the spirits ruling in the air, and we saw, felt and experienced something of the reality of these spirits. As Paul wrote on one occasion, "We are not contending against flesh and blood, but against the principalities, against the powers, against the world rulers of this present darkness, against the spiritual hosts of wickedness in the heavenly places."

We came to feel these realities very much through several heavily burdened people. Oswald, who came from Weissenfels near Naumburg, became a special concern for us. He was a big, brawny man who wore little clothing. His hair was long like a girl's, adorned with a pink ribbon, when he suddenly appeared among us. In those times his appearance was not too conspicuous, but when he suddenly disrobed completely during the midday meal and said cynically, "To the pure everything is pure," we realized that we were dealing with something more than eccentricity. He was sent out of the room immediately. When we called him to the brotherhood meeting later, we became aware that he was a very miserable and tortured man, possessed by impure spirits. Eberhard asked him whether he wanted to be freed from these spirits. To this he answered with a diabolical grin, "You can't do it!" Eberhard said, "But the Church can do it." He ran out of the room, screaming, "I am afraid of this, it has to do with death and the Devil. This means I have to die." He ran away as fast as he could and nobody could catch up with him. And we never heard of him again.

We had a different, much more intensive struggle with a sixteen-year-old girl, Lottchen. Already when she came to us, she had a very peculiar expression on her face. It was noticeable from the beginning that there was something unusual about her. Almost from the start she responded quite positively to our inner life and told us more and more about her childhood and the difficult circumstances of her previous life. Sometimes she had a good expression on her face; at other times her face revealed something of torment, even of evil.

There were hours when this girl would ask very deep, searching questions, which went far beyond her age; at other times the same mouth would speak quite differently, uttering ugly and hateful words. Eberhard concerned himself very much with her and her need. She was assigned to help me in the work, as it was difficult for her to work just anywhere. On a number of occasions we became aware of the great inner need from which she was suffering, and the whole small circle felt it to be a help when one day Lotte asked to be baptized. A small group was formed to prepare for baptism. The group included Karl Keiderling, who had just returned from a time of absence in Saxony, where he had had a job through the help of our friend the Prince of Schönburg-Waldenburg, who had been our guest in Sannerz. Karl had been asked to establish his marriage with Irmgard on a firm basis before becoming a full member. Heini also took part in this baptism group, and Lotte herself.

When, after a fairly long time of preparation, we talked about the three concerned, it was felt by all that the time was premature for each one of them, and that they should wait

longer. Particularly Lotte came into a great struggle as a
result of this time of serious preparation.

Here I will let Eberhard's words tell of this time when we
all fought for Lotte. In a letter to a group of Christian
publishers he wrote, in April 1926:

Brothers and Friends!

Here in Teichwolframsdorf, where my Emmy and I
are enjoying a short pause to gain strength in the struggle,
I can at last tell you about the cause of the long delay in
the circular letter. Certainly there is no excuse for my
having let the circular letter wait so long, after Emmy had
so faithfully written her contribution the same day that the
letter arrived. Perhaps it would have been right to send
the letter on immediately without any contribution from
me. But I believed that I ought to share something of
what was moving me so strongly. And I kept hoping that
any day I would be given this task and be free to do it.
I will now write to you the reason why this was not
possible until now. I ask you to understand that one needs
an urge and a calling to be able to do this. I am sure
that through it we can come very close to one another.
This winter we have had to go through hard times of
struggle. I did not want to burden you with it until the
greatest difficulties were over. We came so close to each
other at Stolberg and made such a firm bond there that
we must openly give one another insight into the decisive
experiences in our fight. How I am looking forward to
being with you again in June.

There have been two difficult tasks and struggles for
us this winter. One was economic. The existence of our
common life in these hard times was at stake. This tough
fight alone could have used up all our strength; it went

on in all areas of our work. Except for the year 1922, we never had to fight so hard for the continued existence of our life witness.

Yet the other task in the fight was considerably more difficult, more fateful. I can only indicate the essentials of this crisis in broad outline, since the details cannot be told here. We found ourselves in a spiritual struggle such as we had never known before, against dark powers which developed a force unknown to us until then. Previously in our life in Sannerz we had come to know the demonic powers of today and what power they have over people in these days. But never had we come across this power in such a frightening way as this winter. We had to be right there day and night, until after weeks of wrestling the main strength of the Hostile Power was broken.

It was a great help to our little life-community that we saw the flashing of the power which conquers demons, coming not only from Blumhardt, but even more from the early Christians of the first centuries. The sinister manifestations and terrifying blasphemies, the storming and raving, the taking possession of the tormented person by the Evil Power, the attack on the faith and on the believers—all this can be broken only by the Name of Jesus Christ, by witnessing to His history, from the virgin birth to His words and deeds and to His crucifixion and resurrection. These things can be broken only by the power and authority of the Holy Spirit. Men can do nothing here. Care of the individual soul is completely inadequate. The Church alone is empowered and authorized to command these spirits, no matter how small a handful of devoted believers represents it. The Demonic Power, on the other hand, becomes anxious and fearful.

The possessed person expresses this cowardly fear by physical collapse, by fleeing and hiding. The important thing now is to hold on, to believe in Christ and to banish the Evil Power completely through Him, until the possessed person is freed and can himself now call upon Christ. After we had experienced this victory by God—it was the most memorable New Year's Eve—there were some among us who came to a faith in God and an awareness of human smallness such as they had not known previously. It became clearer than ever to us that the main thing was not one small individual human being and his salvation, but the struggle for supremacy between two spiritual powers; it is the conflict between God and Satan; between the only good power, the power of the Holy Spirit, and the evil forces of the demons. We became more certain than ever that the Kingdom of God *is Power*.

These struggles were drawn out over a period of weeks and often took up the nights as well, so that afterwards we were very tired. The three months that followed were almost more difficult. This person, who had undergone such unspeakable torment, now had to be guided to a Biblical faith, to the faith of the Church, and in spite of all that had happened, this was not yet assured. We now had to struggle with doubts and misgivings in our own circle, which had held on so courageously in the days of the great fight. This was due particularly to the fact that the person in question, who was now entrusted to us in a special way, had relapses. True, these relapses did not show the same symptoms of being possessed, but they did have distressing consequences, the effects of a bad spirit. Thus attention was focused too much on this person and diverted to a painful degree from the Great Love.

In this situation now it is important that our little Church be strengthened in the Biblical faith through hours of quiet, so that Christ may purify us and prepare us as He wants to do. He wants to bring into reality the greatness of God, the purity of the life of His Church and the complete love for Him and for all men; this must be believed, it must be lived. We stand here in the midst of a struggle, a becoming; we stand at the beginning of a new time.

We now ask you from our hearts to have patience with us in this situation and this task of ours, and, above all, to continue to support us with your practical help and your prayers that God may fan the flames of the decisive struggle in His Church everywhere and lead it to victory.

Looking forward with joy to our meeting, in faithful fellowship of the struggle and in unity of conviction,

your brother,<br>
Eberhard Arnold

P.S. To show that my long delay in writing was not due to indifference, I am sending copies of this letter to the brothers who cannot receive it right away. You will all realize that the trust of our friendship requires that this information be strictly confidential. For I have been urged to come out with this only by this trusting friendship and by your so richly justified expectation of the circular letter. Things of this nature should be received in quiet and silence as much as possible.

During the days of this very intensive struggle against dark powers we were reminded again and again of Blumhardt's struggle. It had been our belief that Lotte would become a co-worker with us in our life together in the same way as Gottliebin had been in the life of Blumhardt. This was not given, however. She stayed with us one more year. Struggles of this kind did not occur again, and she tried, in a way, to live with us. After she left us she came back from time to time, once with a child. Later, during the time of the Nazis, she again came to us with the child, when she was persecuted by the Gestapo because she was fighting for the proletariat on the side of the Communists. She then was put into a concentration camp. We did not hear of her again after that.

The song that was given to us during this time had much to say to us in those days which were so tremendously stirring:

> To sail through deadly peril,
> Imprisoned by dark fate;
> With multitudes to journey,
> By mortal powers racked—
> Despairing, without mercy—
> In gloom of darkness damned—
> Is damage without rescue;
> The passage way is blocked.

> There, from the distant shore shines
> A light, an eye, a star.
> It calls from shore to vessel,
> It strikes the inmost heart.
> The call new life awakens,
> It stirs the depths of birth,
> The withered limbs are lifting,
> Arising to new life.

> The multitudes arising
> Get free from pangs of death,
> To light once more they're sailing,
> Their ranks are closed once more.
> Their bond is new in oneness,

The ring is round and firm.
The hand washed pure with water
Now firmly holds the ring.

Anew the Voice is calling,
The call: Sail into death!
Sail into death, yet living,
Protected now for life!
The multitudes with courage
Sail into death's abode,
Sail into Hell and darkness
To conquer e'en the tomb.

New life from death is 'wakened,
For God breaks stone and grave!
The boulder now is lifted,
The weakest are made strong.
They who were numb in deadness
Now force and blaze the trail.
The call is carried forward,
It is their life and soul.

# THE RHÖN BRUDERHOF

SOON OTHER EVENTS happened in our life which were to occupy us fully. People came and went. The door was open for entering and for leaving. Strange kinds of people came looking for a place of refuge with us. A young woman who had run away from her husband looked for shelter with us. A young man, wanted by the police, suddenly vanished behind a cupboard during one of our communal meals, when through the window he saw the police approaching. A young girl made the trip to us from Berlin because of an unhappy love affair to which her father, a doctor, had put an end. There were various reasons attracting people to Sannerz, not always of the deepest nature.

Our Sannerz house had become too small and we had to look around for a new place, even though we had no money for one. We made a number of trips to this end. It was just at that time that several young men arrived in our house who wanted to help us with our work of building up. Among them were Alfred, Arno, Hans, Fritz, and Kurt, who stayed and were to become a good help later. Others helped out for a time but got tired of the hardships of the life. It was also at this time that many "brothers of the road" (tramps) stayed with us. Yes, many were forced to the road in these years because they could not find work, the aftermath of the years of war and revolution. On account of the prevailing conditions there was increased dissatisfaction among the people, even more so because food still was very hard to come by. As always, we had at this time to fight particularly against the demon of Mammon. It was vital for us to take up this fight again and again. This was, and still is, a struggle which demands our unyielding courage and resistance.

In spite of these difficulties we set out to look for a new place. After a while we were told about the Sparhof, a large farm situated in a very poor area in the Rhön mountains. Here the very poorest of peasants lived, and they did not enjoy a very good reputation in these parts. This did not frighten us. It was a time of much wandering, and we were looking for the poor. Somebody said to us at the time, "So you want to go where the foxes say good night to each other." Anyway, the largest homestead, the Hansehof (the Sparhof consisted of seven farmsteads altogether), was unoccupied at the time. Ownership had changed hands many times because of debt and death. Even though the buildings were in a poor and dilapidated state and the fields were neglected, the asking price was 26,000 marks ($6,500), and there were strings attached, such as a couple there who had the right to live on the place. Yet it was the only place among those up for sale at the time which seemed to hold possibilities for us.

After several of us had seen the place, very much run down as it was, we had a meeting of the brotherhood. That the farmstead was only a few miles away from Sannerz was a point in its favor, considering the ease of moving. The neglected condition of the small farm of about seventy-five acres did not worry us too much; we felt young and were looking forward to building up this place, to setting up a "monument" of communal life, as Eberhard expressed it. *But* where were we to find the 10,000 marks ($2,500) downpayment? Where were we to find the money to rebuild and enlarge the main house, which was quite uninhabitable? There were about forty to fifty of us then who had to find room in this farmhouse. Yes, this beginning was exciting for us! We decided in the brotherhood to take the step in faith and buy the place!

Eberhard and I were sent to make the necessary arrangements. After we had spoken with the owners and their heirs we traveled to Fulda in the hope that it would be possible to sign a contract of sale before a notary public. Else and I sat in the Café Hesse waiting for Eberhard. He came to take us to sign our names. I said I had not thought that we would sign already on this day, as we would have to deposit the 10,000 marks downpayment only ten days later. To this Eberhard replied in a matter-of-fact way, "But this is a step taken in faith!" Then we went together and signed the contract.

This was in the fall of 1926. We had, of course, informed a number of our friends of the need for buying a new place, but when we did this we could not think of anybody who would be able to give us this sum of 10,000 marks. Yet one or two days before the payment was due we had the 10,000 marks in our hands, through the kindness of our friend the Prince of Schönburg-Waldenburg. The jubilation and gratefulness which was felt by the whole community! All were called together and we sang one song of praise after another.

Now it was a question of tackling the practical issues. Whereas the practical things like the conveyance of title and other formalities had still to be settled, we talked in the brotherhood about the first steps to be taken. One thing that had to be done was to bring in the harvest, particularly the potatoes.

This was to be done by the children with their teachers. We were badly in need of potatoes as our staple food, for we had no money.

Further, a building troop was to be formed, to be led by Georg Barth whose training had something to do with making drawings for building work. The farm work (including the ploughing) was to be taken in hand by Adolf Braun, later by Arno Martin, who came to us in December. The publishing work and the children's community were to remain in Sannerz for the time being, until accommodation should become available as the result of the remodeling and construction work. Adolf and Martha were asked to be responsible for the new place, the Rhön Bruderhof, as house parents. To help them, Gertrud Ziebarth (later Dyroff) was also sent. Gertrud served the community faithfully until the end of her life. She died in 1939 after the birth of her third son, Bernhard.

The first group to move was the children from twelve to fourteen, for the potato harvest. It was November already, and a cold, sharp, north wind was howling. Though it was foggy and rainy, the work had to be done speedily, before the hard frost came. Those who were working in the field the whole day were strengthened with hot drinks prepared for them by Martha, Moni or me. We had gone over there with the children. For the nights we put down some straw in one of the rooms, for the children and adults to sleep on. We also installed a small iron stove and, as we did not have a proper chimney at the time, we simply stuck the stovepipe out through a hole in the window. In this way we were able to have at least a little warmth. Whenever the children's hands and feet grew too cold we would interrupt the work to dance with them in a circle. It was a joyful if rather rough beginning which we experienced with the children.

At the same time the fields were being ploughed to get the land into shape for the coming spring and summer. The farm tools were also in poor condition and had to be repaired. For this Fritz Kleiner, the blacksmith, was just the right man.[1] The building team, led by Georg, consisted of young friends from both the youth movement and the working class movement. Building was by no means easy, for we had neither money nor building material of any kind. We first had to cut down trees in the forest. As the green timber was unsuitable for building we had to exchange the felled trees for seasoned timber in Veitsteinbach, our nearest village. Clay for the air-dried bricks, which we made ourselves, had to be fetched from Mittelkalbach, about an hour and a quarter's trip downhill and a correspondingly longer trip uphill. All carting had to be done with our old horses, which we had acquired together with the farmstead. During the day these horses had to plough or move furniture and equipment up from Sannerz; during the night they had to haul up loads of material for the building. No wonder that one of the horses died very soon after, and another one became ill—simply stopped and refused to carry on.

The light young horses of the Trakehnen breed, which we bought a little later, were also much overtaxed. They were meant to be used for the transport of people and for mission work in the villages around. For this purpose we had a light buggy, equipped for transporting and exhibiting books and pamphlets. This was thought of as a temporary arrangement, as we were thinking of getting a trailer for this work at a later date. The Trakehners were used for the trips to the various railroad stations—Sterbfritz, a trip of about an hour and a half, or Neuhof, a little farther away. Yes, we even

[1] Fritz Kleiner died in Primavera, Paraguay, in December 1947.

used the light coach to go all the way to Fulda, a distance of some twenty miles, since often we simply did not have the money to pay for train tickets. For any cash needed in town we had first to sell our books or pamphlets, or small pieces of craft work made by us, such as candlesticks, little Nativity scenes, or bookmarks made from galalith, an ivory-like milk product.

I still remember one of these trips which we made a short time before Christmas in our little buggy. Else (Tata) was driving. We had just enough money on us to buy a cup of coffee to warm ourselves up on the way. But alas, our little horse Freia went on strike halfway to Fulda. She just lay down on the road, and neither our encouraging words nor our whip-cracking did any good. Our horse just would not get up again. Only when we gave her *our coffee* to drink did she graciously get up on her feet and pull us the remaining twelve miles to Fulda. Yes, beginnings are always hard! However, courage was given to us again and again. Humor helped us in bearing many things, and difficult moments were often lightened by it.

No wonder the young men working in the building often were at the end of their strength; the food was so poor! Actually everything was in short supply. Meat was very scarce, and the rations of bread, fat, and sugar were inadequate. Our best item of food was still the potatoes, but they had suffered from frost because of the late harvest, and this gave them a sweet taste. We had some very tough beef from old cows, and some sauerkraut which had fermented and of which we could have our fill. But there was no fat in the diet. The few provisions we were able to purchase had to be divided between those who were still in Sannerz and the group which had moved to the new place. And the people there, who were doing hard work in cold weather, were especially hungry. On occasion they would kill a "roof hare" (cat) because they were so very hungry.

Every week Eberhard and I spent two or three days on the farm; we drove there by sleigh. Several times it happened that we were not able to find the way because of the fog and snow. We drove around in circles on the plateau until one of the builders or one of the men working in the fields heard our shouting. We had lost the road on account of the deep snow. The worst situations arose when it was completely dark and we could not see anything at all.

Our help was needed in many ways—giving encouragement, having personal talks, straightening out quarrels or standing up against a lack of understanding for the difficult situation we were in. Cheerful and humorous songs often helped us to overcome the difficulties which, for the most part, were quite understandable. The songs of hope, "Dismal, drear dawned mankind's ice age" and "Through the gateway of the age," were sung many times, also a number of socialist songs, such as the one with the lines:

> We're bound by love, we're bound by need
> To fight for freedom and for bread.

Yes, the idealism of these young co-workers was great indeed. However, it was not always sufficient to overcome all these hardships. Thus several left us, not only as a result of the outward difficulties, but also because of the severe inner demands which, in actual fact, were made of all; because of the radicalism entailed in following Jesus: "Whoever of you does not renounce all that he has cannot be my disciple."

During all this time the school and educational work continued. The children rehearsed a Christmas play. Between Christmas and the New Year we had a conference of the

Free German Youth movement which Edgar and Ernestine Koch, as well as Hedwig Eichbauer, attended. One day we walked up from Sannerz to the Rhön Bruderhof and held our meetings there. The publishing work also continued as much as possible. The division into two groups was no easy matter. Misunderstandings often arose between the two groups. They were resolved each time by personal talks and common experiences. It just is a mystery, this life in common, this working together.

We were very glad, therefore, when we had reached the point in the summer when it became possible for the children (there were about fifteen at the time) to make the move, so that all of us came together at the Rhön Bruderhof. It was a happy day, our exodus from Sannerz; the children left first, with quite a variety of vehicles! Even then some of the children, with Georg, had to move into a barn toward Gundhelm, as we were still short of rooms. But what did it matter? It was summer anyhow, and we liked to live with nature as much as possible. Later, in the fall, the publishing house also moved, after Sannerz had celebrated the engagement of Georg and Moni. This was the first engagement in the community! It was an occasion for lots of fun-making and joking, especially by the young people. On the morning after the engagement had been announced the doors and windows were decorated with red hearts, and additional lines were spontaneously added to the song, "Who comes up the meadow way?" This and other songs were sung by those who were young at the time, such as Arno, Hans, Fritz, etc.

The wedding itself was celebrated about two months later at the Rhön Bruderhof. It was the first wedding in the community, too! In spite of our great poverty—noodle soup was the main dish—this was a very joyful celebration together. Red Christmas candles burned on a seven-armed candlestick which Georg himself had made, and the whole celebration, with coffee and Christmas cake, was very festive, as the preceding wedding ceremony itself had been. Guests had also been invited. Georg's sister Hilde came, and Hermann Buddensieg, editor of the magazine of the Free German Youth, *Der Rufer zur Wende* ("The Crier for the New Era").

The questions put to the young couple were taken from Zinzendorf and made a deep impression on all who were present.

"What special mystery does a Church of God have?"

"Marriage."

"Of what is the mystery of marriage an example?"

"It is an example of Christ and the Church."[2]

Carrying a red candle in her hand, Emi-Margret recited for the first time the poem by Methodius the Martyr, "From on High, O virgins," with the chorus,

> I dedicate myself to Thee,
> And carrying the shining lamp,
> I go to meet Thee, O Bridegroom.

Rose Meyer (now Kaiser) recited the hymn by Zinzendorf, "We love each other truly." I am especially fond of the verse,

> O Church, give thy love completely and ardently,
> With consecrated powers;
> For God chose thee from eternity for love.
> It is fitting that thy heart embrace
> Both those who love thee and hate thee.

During the wedding ceremony and the lovemeal[3] Moni

---

[2] Zinzendorf, *Über Glauben und Leben,* p. 102.

[3] A special communal meal to symbolize the love which Jesus said His followers should have for each other.

wore a white corduroy dress. She looked quite young in this, with the myrtle wreath in her hair, even though she was a good deal older than Georg.

After all these festivities, which took place on December 3 and 4 of 1927, Georg and Moni, full of joy, left for Würzburg. They spent a few days in this beautiful old town, so full of memories and of reverence for Mary, just during this time of Advent and preparation for Christmas.

This journey was made possible only through a good deal of sacrifice, as our finances were strained and we were heavily indebted. It was just in those days that notes became due and had to be extended. On the evening before the wedding, our Tata had to work for this right to the last hour when the festivities were already beginning. She just managed to be in time for the celebration—exhausted by all this great rush.

The Christmas time which followed was one which always remained in our memories as a special experience for us all. First there was the communal experience of Christ's coming on earth. There was also the Christmas play, in which Georg played the part of Simeon and I took the part of Hannah. There were the old and new Christmas songs; and there was the hope which filled our hearts for the coming Final Advent when peace, joy and justice shall reign for all men!

After the Christmas days, until after the New Year began, we met in the brotherhood every day at teatime to take counsel together about what was old and what was to become new! In this way certain matters were cleared and put behind us which had been disturbing, between individuals and in the whole circle of the community. Thus a time of clarification was given to us during this interim period, the time "between the years," as we called it. We looked back upon the past and ahead and forward into the future, at this time of our new beginning when all of us were together at the Rhön Bruderhof. In later years, when the farm or building work was very pressing, we would say to each other, "Well now, let's talk about all this under the Christmas tree." Again and again in our life together it became evident that such times of clarification were necessary. After Eberhard's return from his American journey to the Hutterites, this was done during the time of preparation for the Lord's Supper at Easter.

Just during this time "between the years" we experienced the death of little Ursula Keiderling. Wet wood had been drying near the stove, and the little child, eleven months old, had been left alone in the room for a short time. When her mother, Irmgard, had left the room, the little one had been sitting in her bed playing. When she returned the room was full of smoke and the child was breathing heavily. The doctor diagnosed pneumonia, and the little girl died the following evening, on December 30. The time we had spent at her bedside, more than twenty-four hours, had been filled with great concern and anxiety.

This death brought us all very close together, especially with the parents, Karl and Irmgard. The body of the little child lay in the publishing office, at her side a small Christmas tree with candles burning. We sang for her the cradle songs of Christmas—"Still, still, still, for Jesus goes to sleep"; "Let's rock the infant tender." A verse from the song, "On the mountain the wind bloweth wild," became of special significance to us:

> The Child, waking, holdeth toward Heaven His hands.
> The angels are singing, rejoicing all lands,
> For death now is vanquished, and pain and sin's might;
> Beloved and praised be God in the Height!

On the morning of December 31 Eberhard and I traveled to Fulda to ask for permission from the authorities to bury the little body on our Bruderhof land. However, on this last day of the year, with New Year's Day following, it was too late, as a further journey to Kassel was required in order to get the necessary license. So we then carried our little Ursula to the Catholic cemetery in Veitsteinbach, where we were allowed to have our own burial meeting.

Thus the end of the year 1927 was a very serious time for us, and we felt that eternity was very close.

> In the midst of life we are
> By dark death surrounded.
> Whom shall we seek to give us help,
> That mercy we may find?
> Thee alone, O God!

Hans and Fritz felt very much spoken to by the seriousness of the hour. On New Year's Eve they made known their decision to give their whole lives from now on to our common task. This was a particular joy and encouragement for the year 1928!

Arno had taken the same step a short while before. Thus we now had three young brothers who were able to carry something on their shoulders. Since 1922 there had been more women than men among us who wanted to give their lives completely to the cause. Among them was our dear Katrin, who came at this time with her baby Anna; she was a peasant woman from the neighborhood—the only one from the neighborhood to come to us—and was soon completely united with us. Karl Keiderling had come, and so had Adolf Braun, both married men with families, and also Alfred Gneiting. Georg joined in 1925 and Kurt Zimmermann in the summer of 1928.

There were always transient young men, or "travelers," who stayed for longer or shorter periods, such as Karlchen Gail. After the experience of this New Year's Eve it happened frequently that new people felt the call to give their lives on New Year's Eve and expressed this in the meeting. We felt the importance of such decisions very strongly, and the new step into the New Year was taken in courage and in faith.

The years of 1928 and 1929 brought many a struggle, against the devil of Mammon and against the powers of illness. We had hardly started at the Rhön Bruderhof when the whole property was threatened with being sold at auction by court order. Notes became due which we were not able to pay. One, two, even three or more of us were constantly traveling about in an effort to get these notes extended; this was very expensive because of the high interest rates. Mr. Schreiner, the sheriff, came nearly every Friday to impound either a piece of furniture, a cow, or a hog. This meant that he glued a "cuckoo" (the German eagle pictured on the sticker) on the piece of equipment or above the animal seized. Hence Eberhard's joking remark that Mr. Schreiner would not need to wait a year to become a member of the brotherhood, as he had been our constant guest, every Friday. On one occasion things went so far that the compulsory sale of the whole place was prevented only at the last minute! All this had a paralyzing effect on our working strength but *never* on the joy and certainty for the cause entrusted to us. We simply felt assured that this cause *had* to continue and go forward.

During this time our Tata became very ill again. The doctors gave her only a few days to live. Yet when we prayed for her together, she recovered very quickly, and immediately took up again her important task as secretary. She just could not and would not take care of herself!

Just at this particular time, in the year 1928, we experienced a great deal, for we became absorbed in the history of sixteenth-century Anabaptism. We were especially enthusiastic about the early beginnings of the Hutterian Brothers because it corresponded in so many ways to our own beginning. We read about the beginnings of their common life, their methods of education, their economy and the accounts of their martyrs. We were very deeply moved by all this because we felt strongly that here was the same Spirit who had called us to the same witness and life in our own age. I remember Fritz speaking up after a meeting upstairs in the publishing office. "What exactly is hindering us from uniting with the Hutterian Brothers?" he asked. This happened soon after we had heard that they were still in existence and were living in America.

Consequently a document was drawn up stating that we were called to the same life of following Christ to which the Brothers had been called four hundred years ago, and that we desired to be united with them. The letter was addressed to Elias Walter at the Stand Off Bruderhof near Macleod, Alberta. We eagerly awaited his reply, which did not arrive for a long time. We felt somewhat sobered down when at first only a few booklets written by Andreas Ehrenpreis arrived. However, a little later a short reply to our letter arrived. Eberhard and I and the early members never wanted to be the "founders" of a work of our own; we believed that we belonged within the ranks of those who strove to live the same kind of life in past centuries and in our own time. Therefore we belonged to these Brothers in a particular way.

As a result of the correspondence that followed, Eberhard was invited to visit the Hutterian Brothers in America. The journey took place in 1930, after many letters had been exchanged with Elias Walter. This will be told later.

There are other things to tell about which happened at the Rhön Bruderhof during its early years. The time of real awakening in the great post-war movement had subsided more and more, as Eberhard had put it at the Whitsun Conference in Wallroth in 1923 when he spoke of "the funeral of the movement."[4] At that time he was contradicted on all sides, though later this sentence was often quoted. However, this spirit of awakening was still alive in Germany in some youth circles, such as the Neu-Sonnefeld Youth and the Eisenach Youth; in Switzerland, Holland, and England, too, we came more and more into contact with such groups.

Many a settlement had collapsed and disbanded as a result of disillusionment, erotic problems, and vegetarianism; frequently also because of a radicalism which could not be carried out. Often the reason was that everyone wanted to have a work of his *own*. Some also believed that freedom, which was an important concern to many, consisted in everybody doing his job whenever he felt like it, and that nobody should be asked by anybody else to do a job. This was the way the word of the "inner must" was understood. "We have worked under the lash far too long."—"We did not join a settlement to be called or ordered to work by others!"—"We recognize no bosses here." The question of freedom was a great theme in the evening meetings we had with our guests.

In those years we were also visited by several representatives of Russian Communism. Some of them called us "noble communists" (*Edelkommunisten*). Others left us, full of indignation, and said to us, "When Communism seizes power, you will be the first to hang on the gallows." Eberhard in particular strongly represented that we could have nothing to do with violence if we wanted to go the way of Jesus, but that socialism

[4] Report of the 1923 Whitsun Conference in *Neuwerk* for 1923.

nevertheless had something to say to the world, because the world Churches and the so-called Christians had joined forces with wealth and with the worldly State and had thus become a stumbling block to many serious-minded people. "If the disciples were silent, the very stones would cry out."

The last line of "Brothers, to the sun and freedom," a song originating in socialist circles, was rewritten. Instead of the words, "Holy the last battle," we sang the words, "Holy the power of love!"

At that time many guests from nationalistic circles began visiting us. With them we discussed the question of "national interest above self-interest" (*Gemeinnutz vor Eigennutz*) and "the nation as a community" (*Volksgemeinschaft*). Sometimes we had considerable argument with them, even though we looked for ideas held in common. What Hitler was to become later can be understood only in the context of the idealism which was alive among many seeking people at that time, but also, and this in a special way, in the context of the hardships under which the German people were laboring then, many years after the war had ended. Foodstuffs were scarce and prices were high, largely because the former German colonies were occupied by the victor nations and thus all imported goods were too expensive, including tea, coffee and other, more vital items of food. At this point I must pay a tribute to the help given by the Quakers to schools and hospitals, orphanages and old people's homes.

Another situation that weighed heavily on the people was the high rate of unemployment, through which many young people became ruined on the streets of the big cities. Added to this there was the inflation during the years 1923–1924, when the currency became completely devaluated. Paper money was issued going into millions and billions of marks.

A sum of money which today could still buy something of value, was hardly enough to buy a pound of margarine tomorrow. For example, we still had an old family heirloom, an antique mahogany cupboard with glass doors in the Biedermeier style, filled with valuable old Meissen chinaware — hand-painted cups, plates and vases. We decided in a brotherhood meeting to take the cupboard to an antique dealer in Frankfurt. He sold each piece separately; yet by the time we received the money it had become valueless. As a result of all these hardships, people began already in those years to yearn for a leader, a dictator, who would restore order, whether he came from the right or from the left!

Our children's community kept on growing. Children were brought to us who did not have a real home. Among them were Karl-Heinz Schultheiss, Edgar Zimmermann, Richard Götz and others. One day a policeman came and asked us whether we would accept a child from the "wandering folk" (the gypsies). He had found the child in a sack or a rucksack hanging from a tree at the roadside, with a note attached saying, "Whoever finds this child may keep it." We took in the little boy, Erhardt, who was about two years old. Adolf and Martha Braun took him into their family together with their two little girls, Gertrud and Elfriede. He was a poor, neglected little boy, plagued by scabies and lice. But soon we were able to see how well little Erhardt developed, responding to good care. As he grew up he was very much liked by both children and adults. When he became older those who looked after him noticed a certain restlessness in him, an urge to rove and ramble. However, he never ran away for long. Unfortunately, during the Hitler time the boy was suddenly taken away by his father, a dark, gypsy type of man, who turned up on a bicycle and produced an official paper to the effect that he was to take the boy with him. We never saw him again.

We had a similar experience with "Ulala," who was given into our care by gypsies when he was still a baby. Moni in particular took care of him. He also was taken away one day, after he had grown to early boyhood. At first he lived with his family in a trailer in the outskirts of Fulda, a very poor district. We visited him there in an effort to get him back to us, but in vain. Later he was placed in a Catholic institution, and we were told that he died there.

It was during this time too that our dear Walla was brought to us by his mother because of unhappy family circumstances. He was part of our family, and Tata looked after him faithfully. His age was a year and a half when he first came to us. He went back to his mother for a short time; then Else brought him back and adopted him, because the Roman Catholic Church made claims on him. Tata took care of him as long as she was able. Later, in the summer of 1931 when Tata became so ill, our thirteen-year-old daughter Monika looked after him, providing for him, mending, knitting, reading stories and singing songs to him—the greatest joy to them both.

These are only a few examples of what we experienced with children in those years.

In the meantime our children were growing up, and we decided after careful consideration in the brotherhood that each one of them should have a training outside the Bruderhof, if possible. For one thing, we wanted them to learn something worthwhile that they could put to good use at home or elsewhere; then too, we did not want any half-hearted sojourners on the narrow way we had taken, not even in our own families or among the children who were brought up by us.

Emi-Margret, then, entered a Froebel training school for kindergarten teachers, in Thale, in the Harz Mountains. Hardi went to a Hermann Lietz School, a modern school similar to a preparatory school but including training in farming and craft work. Hansemann (Hans Grimm) was apprenticed to a carpenter for a three-year period. We continued in this way until 1933, when the Nazi Government put an end to it all.

To our great joy, in 1928 a kindergarten teacher joined us—our dear Gretel (now Gneiting).

During the early years at the Rhön Bruderhof all of us who lived there were closely bound up with farming and with nature. However, this small and at first run-down farm did not provide a sufficient basis for even the simplest livelihood for our community and its helpers and guests. We had only enough grain for bread to last us about six months, from harvest time until spring. It was difficult to buy bread, as most of the time we had no money. I still remember the occasion when a guest donated fifty marks ($12). Immediately one of our youngsters was dispatched to the neighboring village to buy bread! Often we were given a loaf of bread as a birthday present instead of cake, and many preferred this. In a letter to our guests written in 1928, which they were all asked to read, we requested that each guest who insisted on having bread should provide his own, as our harvest was insufficient and sometimes we had none. That we had no bread was hard for some to understand. After all, bread is the basic food for people—and how we had missed it during the First World War!

A verse from the Matthias Claudius song, "We plough the fields and scatter," was rewritten so that instead of the lines,

> He gives the cattle pasture
> And to our children bread,

we sometimes sang,

> He gives the children pasture
> And to our cattle bread.

That was a time when we often ate wild spinach, while the cows were fed as much grain concentrate as possible, so that the children got the milk they needed.

The garden vegetables, planted by our gardener Walter from the time he joined in 1929 on, ripened late because of the high elevation of the Rhön Bruderhof and the prevailing cold winds. (Walter had come from the Religious Socialist Movement in Switzerland.) The potatoes, too, came to an end in the spring, and therefore our food was very poor during the summer months. It was a consolation, though, to be able to watch things grow and to look forward to harvest time. After the first hog was slaughtered, many of us got an upset stomach because we were not used to that kind of food anymore.

No wonder, then, that the health of several was poor. Our Tata, who had lost half of her stomach through an operation, also suffered from tuberculosis of the lungs. Emi-Margret, who was only seventeen at the time, contracted her first mild attack of tuberculosis. She recovered after a time of rest and as a result of better diet. Thus she was able to start her kindergarten training in the fall of 1928. Also others who were not so strong, like Luise, suffered from the prevailing shortage of good, nutritious food.

To improve our long-term food situation we decided in the fall of 1932 to plant windbreaks against the cold winds by planting a spruce and larch wood on the hill, where only heather was then growing. We did this with the help of a work camp composed of young Baptists. This was, of course, not for immediate help, but to improve the food production in the future. We also planted fruit trees on our land, such as cherries, plums and apples. When I returned to the Rhön Bruderhof from Primavera, Paraguay, in 1955, after being away nineteen years, I found a wonderful little forest there, with tall spruces, also around the place on the hill where we had our burial ground since 1932. The windbreak was fully grown and a great help to the present farmer there. However, the fruit trees were neglected and in bad shape.

In spite of the great poverty of those years our children's community was growing constantly, and it became necessary to build a children's house. Through the good offices of a friendly and understanding local official, District Administrator von Gagern, we were able to secure a favorable long-term building loan from the government which made it possible for us to begin with the building. What a tremendous event it was to be able to break ground for this building, which was to replace an old, dilapidated shed or barn! All of us, the whole community, took a lively interest in this work. Georg prepared the plans and Fritz carried through the actual building operation. The first house to be built by us on our own land! What a joy to see the walls go up in spite of the great shortage of cash to buy the necessary materials!

At the dedication ceremony of the children's house the president of the Kassel administration attended, as well as the district magistrate from Fulda. It took place on the very same day for which the court sale of the property had been originally decreed. (This had been averted, however, when we suddenly and completely unexpectedly received the sum of 5,000 Swiss francs, or $1,250, helping us to get over the worst of the crisis.) It was during the dedication celebration for the new house that we for the first time sang the song, *Wir hatten gebauet ein stattliches Haus* ("We built up a house that was stately and strong"). Certainly, the last verse of this song seemed at that time very remote:

> What though the house be ruined,
> We count not the loss;
> The Spirit lives among us
> And our stronghold is God.

We realized clearly that we were shouldering a big burden when we bought this run-down, dilapidated farmstead, to which we soon added a smaller adjoining farm, the "Lower Farm." We had to buy livestock, erect new living quarters to house the growing number of people, equip the workshops, and even start a small printing shop of our own, with a hand press. The school, too, needed improvement and expansion. For all this, money was needed. It was our plan to buy all seven farmsteads of the Sparhof eventually. In this way we believed we could accommodate and support two to three hundred people.

In the fall of 1928, Eberhard said in a talk to the brotherhood (still extant in our archives) that one day our movement would grow considerably. Eberhard said he could visualize all manner of people coming—men of industry, professional people, workers, teachers, washerwomen and the very poorest of every description. All of them would want to live in community, and he could see a great procession of people approaching; it was our task to make room for them and to build for them.

At first I could not grasp this at all. I just imagined the Sparhof, with its possibilities for 200 to 250 people, as yet undeveloped, and I just could not see how we would ever be able to find room for the "thousands" of people Eberhard visualized as coming. Even to develop the Sparhof seemed to me a very difficult goal to reach. When Eberhard and I talked this question over together it became clear that Eberhard had spoken of the future of the cause without having in mind any particular geographical limits, while I had felt the way it is expressed in one of our popular hunting songs: "I do not know your high, wide jumps." I also said this in the brotherhood. Our whole circle shared in this little incident, and during the following mealtime the verse was sung over and over again with the chorus, "Hussassa, tralala, I do not know your high, wide jumps." The two of us, Eberhard and I, made use of the opportunity of a visit to Eberhard's mother in Breslau to talk this whole question over together thoroughly, and I often look back with joy to these lively talks we had during our walks in the Scheitnig Park, where we came to complete understanding and agreement.

While we were having all these experiences that I have tried to describe, we read a good deal about the moving times in past centuries, especially during the Reformation time. All this appealed to us very much, and not only to us but also to many others, especially young people. It was the communal spirit as it expressed itself in buildings, art and writings. We felt deeply happy when reading about the peace-loving Anabaptists of the sixteenth century, such as Hans Denck, Balthasar Hubmaier, and others. We also learned to understand Thomas Münzer as an outstanding fighter for the suffering people in his time; he was compared with the contemporary working-class movement and the Religious Socialists: Hermann Kutter, Leonhard Ragaz, Karl Barth and others in our own time, and their struggle against inequality and injustice among men. Yet we did not feel that the answer was simply a matter of protesting, though we also did protest, by participating in marches against political murder, for instance, when Walter Rathenau and Kurt Eisner were assassinated.

Because we were trying to find a positive answer for our day and age, we were particularly happy when Eberhard brought home books and manuscripts about the Hutterian Brothers from libraries and archives. We felt deeply that the same Spirit had called these Brothers, who had experienced so much martyrdom, and had independently called us to this life.

We were also very much interested in the kind of outward form in which their life was expressed. We read about their "orders," their methods of hygiene of four hundred years ago, their educational practices. Not that we wanted to copy or imitate anything—yet the larger our circle had grown, the more we felt that we were moving in the same direction. Essentially we already had the functions of the various "services" in our own midst. We already had a Servant of the Word, though not by that name; a brother to represent the business and economic side; another to oversee the work; and still another to keep things in good order everywhere. We had a house-mother, a nurse, a sister who helped out in all matters, a school principal and several teachers. These services, however, had grown out of the life, without having been designated or recognized as such.

In our readings we were particularly interested in the cleanliness and order prevailing in the early Hutterian communities and in their schools, which were so good that many noblemen sent their children to these schools.

# AMERICAN JOURNEY

THROUGH EBERHARD'S correspondence with the Hutterites of today in South Dakota and in Manitoba, Canada,
the time for a journey to America came closer and closer. It was
the wish of the little brotherhood of that time to send Eberhard
and perhaps one other person to America for about half a
year. First of all there was the reverence for this 400-year-old
Hutterdom to which we felt, through all we had read, that we
belonged. Then too, there was the great economic need of our
small beginning and the hope that the present-day Hutterians
in America would be glad to share with their fellow-believers
of modern times. Some of the letters that came over to us
from them encouraged us. Others sounded rather disappoint-
ing so that we did not know what would come out of this trip.
Would today's Hutterians of 1929 still be living in the same
Spirit and in the same strength as their forefathers?

So Eberhard prepared for the big journey. Together with
Else (Tata) he was working very intensively on the old testimonies of the Brothers. He edited the Michel Hasel Book,
a collection compiled by Michel Hasel, a Swabian Hutterite
of those times.

On New Year's Eve Eberhard was asked what would be

the greatest moment for him in the new year of 1930. He answered, "The moment when I come home from my trip and can come back again to *our* Bruderhof!"

It is something characteristic of our life that really nothing is won without struggle, and so it was also with this trip to America. As early as the beginning of 1930, Eberhard contracted a severe eye inflammation, especially in the left eye which had become practically blind right at the beginning of our communal life as a result of a detached retina, caused by an accident while chopping wood. Through this the wonderful, loving look of that eye naturally disappeared more and more with the years. These eye inflammations increased despite treatment by the eye doctor, and a considerable worsening took place shortly before Eberhard's departure at the end of May. In spite of it, on the evening before leaving he baptized nine of our brothers and sisters in a brook in the woods, the culmination of quite a long preparation time. In spite of many a hard struggle in later years, all of them have remained true to the cause, except for one young man who disappeared shortly afterward. Trautel Dreher died in Primavera in August 1950, leaving her husband Leo and seven young children. The baptism song, "Now come, in love to you we're giving the hands of brotherhood at one," was sung at this baptism for the first time. In the night before Eberhard's departure, Adolf sang at our bedroom door the song of Karl Gerok, "I send you forth! Go out, my twelve, win all the world for me." Tata and I both went with Eberhard as far as Fulda, bringing his baggage—a suitcase containing mostly books and writings, and a rucksack. At Fulda we met our son, Hardi, who had come from Bieberstein.

Since the eye was in very poor condition, Eberhard and I first made one more trip to the eye doctor. The doctor called me into his consultation room and urged that this big journey not be undertaken with the eye in its present condition. On the stairs I said to Eberhard, "But you won't travel like this?" His answer was, "Do let me go! We've always dared a great deal!" Well, he set out. We received many letters from him, though they were a long time on the way. Yes, they all went by ship, and we often felt very much cut off, since it took many weeks to get an answer and only a few times did a cable come.

Naturally we were all eager to know what Eberhard would find in the Hutterian *Bruderhöfe*[1] that had existed 400 years. It is not necessary to write much about this, since the diaries and personal letters are still in existence, as well as his letter to the Hutterian Elders after his trip to America, written in answer to their request to write openly to them about his impressions.

The impressions he received on the Bruderhöfe were quite varied. He felt in a particularly strong way the great love and trust that came to him from the Bruderhöfe, especially from the *Schmiedeleut* ("Smith Group") where he went first. On the other hand he felt very strongly that there was not a real sharing between the Bruderhöfe, with the result that there were rich and well-to-do Bruderhöfe, and also some that were poor and badly in debt. The division into three groups— the Teacher, Darius and Smith Groups—was another thing he found very hard and he felt it was not in keeping with the Spirit, with the love that gives and shares *everything*, the love from which alone Church-community can really arise and continue! The whole question of machinery was another thing that was hard for him; he felt it is really the machine that has man, and not man the machine.

[1] Plural of Bruderhof.

He witnessed again and again to the Hutterians about all these things, especially on the basis of their own early writings. While the Hutterians were very modern already then, in 1930, and had turned completely to modernization in some ways, they were on the other hand very much bound to tradition particularly in the outward forms, which once had their source in living experience. Their style of clothing came from the old Tyrolean peasant costume, though it was somewhat mixed because of their time in Russia, whither they had fled when they were persecuted. Still today they reject musical instruments and photographs; this is a reaction to Catholicism. "Let us sing and play to God *in our hearts!*" they say. They reject not only the organ, piano etc., but even the simplest flutes and shepherd's pipes, fiddles and lutes or guitars. As to pictures they quoted, "Thou shalt make no images!" (But the main thing was forgotten: Thou shalt not worship them!) Already then Eberhard had many a discussion about these things, in which the Elders would not yield.

Of course, our smoking was also a question they raised. Some years earlier this question would not have come up, since smoking, like alcohol, was completely rejected by the youth movement, not as a law, but because it was "Philistinism" (not in keeping with the spirit of the movement). Afterwards, however, smoking was taken up again by one or the other among us. This was the cause of many discussions. Remarkably, the Hutterians were not against alcohol, however, something that we would have understood, since overindulgence in alcohol ruins so many families. (We had no alcohol in any case, as we were so poor.)

Well, all these questions came to us—and brought us many a shock! We especially did not want to place ourselves under laws that were not born out of our living experience. Through the crisis of 1922 and because of the direction taken at that time by the movement toward radical change (which then even broke up) we were on the whole quite isolated, although with the years more and more people joined us. Eberhard's historical view that we belonged to this movement of the Reformation time, and to a certain extent our isolation and financial need, led to our uniting with the Brothers in December 1930. We cherished the hope that new life would break through in the Hutterian movement as it had often done previously.

The same Brothers whom we came to know quite recently, testify that Eberhard's visit at that time brought about a true awakening among the Brothers. And all those whom I met on a later trip to Canada spoke of his visit with deep feeling and thankfulness—after twenty-six years. Some said, too, that they had hoped something new would happen among the Hutterian Church-communities. Besides being in Forest River we were also in Blumengard (J. R. Hofer's Bruderhof) and Spring Valley (where a grandson of Joseph Kleinsasser was Servant of the Word), in Milltown (formerly Joseph Kleinsasser's Bruderhof) and in James Valley (Peter Hofer's Bruderhof) to visit Rahel *Basel*, David *Vetter's* widow.[2]

In the beginning time with Eberhard we tried really to do justice to the origin of the movement of the sixteenth century. We were aware that our own movement came from the youth movement, religious socialism, the worker movement, and Protestant and Catholic movements, which as products of the times also have their defects and do not have eternal meaning in all aspects.

However, some things that went with the uniting were not

[2] The Hutterian term of respectful and loving address for any older Sister, regardless of blood relationship, is *Basel*, for any older Brother, *Vetter*. Both words originally mean "cousin."

easy for us. The Hutterian women's costume with headscarf or *Kopftuch,* which we connected with the youth movement, was not hard for our sisters to accept, especially those who came from the youth movement. On the contrary, they felt something like a fulfillment in the simple peasant costume. In Germany people are quite fond of costumes—Hessian costumes, Bavarian costumes and others are found there. I do not know if today's dress among us is better! However, we did not like the Hutterian men's costume from the beginning—the black or dark gray jackets and trousers, instead of our simple corduroy trousers and jackets. But at that time to wear the same type of clothing was felt as something that united us with the Hutterians.

Giving up pictures, and even more, musical instruments, seemed to us a greater sacrifice. Yet we were willing to give up even these, if it would lead to greater simplicity. But often a picture had so much to say! And the wandering together and sitting together with flutes and guitars, and all the beautiful folk songs and songs of religious awakening—all this seemed to belong to our life. Now this too? Yet what was its eternal value, after all? Such thoughts were often ours during Eberhard's trip to America. Wasn't the unity and oneness of greater worth?

Eberhard's own words, in his letters home to me from North America, will tell best about all he experienced there. Excerpts from these letters, from June 1930 to May 1931, follow here.

*On board S.S. Karlsruhe, June 1 and 2, 1930.*
The eye is supposed to heal by the time I reach New York. I am diligently treating it and have faith in Christ, who wants to make good the inner light as the light of the body and the outer eye for the way. The Kingdom must remain for us.

*Chicago, June 18, 1930.*

At last my eye is so much better that today I have had practically no pain at all. My experience in New York and Scottdale [Pennsylvania] was that the love of the very faithful and very punctual and very earnest Mennonites leaves me no time over and even less strength for writing. Since the eye forced me into bed at every pause for recovery, however short, I have squeezed in an expensive hotel day today, which I am spending in my room, without going out at all ... in order to think and write in quiet to you, to the children, and the whole faithful Bruderhof, and still be able to take care of my eye. ...

The meetings of the Mennonites last many hours and are astonishingly lively even with all the quiet Mennonite seriousness. ... The Bible is read in enormously long sections. The last hour—exactly 60 minutes—was given to me. I took as message to the Mennonites our special theme: The event of Pentecost in Jerusalem with all its consequences. I strongly emphasized Christ's Gospel and then went over to complete love and community in which everything belongs to God and the community of the Spirit. I then told, on their express wish, of my personal development, about you and Halle, Leipzig and Berlin; I witnessed to the Sermon on the Mount and tried to awaken the religious-social conscience. (Afterwards John Horsch said to me that the Mennonites of that time would not all understand such difficult words as "social"! We then agreed that also to our Hutterians I could only show what I meant by the prophets, the rich man and poor Lazarus, the story of the Good Samaritan, etc.) At the end, I told of Sannerz and the Bruderhof and the children's community, emphasizing strongly that I do not have to bear witness to our Bruderhof, but that our

Bruderhof has to bear witness to Jerusalem and the out-pouring of the Holy Spirit with all its consequences. I closed with the very effective song by Emi-Margret [then twelve years old].... At the final words of the song, "And after Him run all who can," I *ran* quickly back to my place, and so joyful laughter closed the talk.... With the Hutterians it will be easier to understand each other, according to John Horsch.... Their Tyrolean-Bavarian dialect will not cause difficulty, but my all too abstract thought-out German may well be difficult for them. Well, perhaps I shall come home as a simple peasant, also in speech.

John Horsch told me many loving and good things about the two visits of the leading Hutterians in Scottdale during the World War [I]. The following brothers were on their way to the Wilson government in Washington with the petition well-known to us: Elias Walter I, Elias Walter II (who at that time was already very influential), the good Joseph Kleinsasser—Elder of the Smith Group, and... David Hofer [3] of Rockport. A Mennonite told about David Hofer, that though they all were brotherly and of one mind in every other way, he, David Hofer, had very stubbornly insisted on being severely and uncompromisingly consistent, with the result that the others had yielded to him on every point except that of resettlement in Canada, against which he had thundered mightily already at that time. He is a particularly pithy character and very hard to influence. The two Elias Walters at that time pushed through the one thing—the emigration to Canada—against his strong will and vigorous opposition; it was done because of the militarization of the United States. David Hofer campaigned hard against them and said he was curious to know how they

[3] Elder of the "Teacher Group" (*Lehrerleut*).

would answer for it on the Day of Judgment that in Canada the children were under the influence of the English state schools for ten months of the year, which was not the case to the same degree in the U.S.A. Who will be proved right in the coming history? . . .

I heard that some Hutterians think that fear for the dollar plays a part in the cool, over-careful treatment of us. David Hofer of Rockport figures that to capitalize [fully] a Bruderhof such as would have to be arranged for us, it would take $250,000, that is, more than a million marks. Well, I can see why they might be worried about that! Let's hope I will succeed in finding the right moderation! But first of all the main thing is the witness and the unity in the Spirit! . . .

Harold Bender wrote a fine letter about the strong impressions which our Bruderhof made on him. He calls us true Baptizers in the sense of the Hutterians, writes about our poverty and community, about our rejection of the liberal idea of progress and about our Biblicism, which is, however, very far removed from pietism. It is a question, he feels, of an honest conviction. He said that . . . with us there are both word and deed, which moved him . . . very much. . . . Since the last day in Scottdale, where I got new atropine through John Horsch's doctor and druggist, the eye is finally getting along better. . . . The baptism [before Eberhard left] was significant, also for the victory of the Spirit over all other spirits, including the painful suffering of the body.

*Tabor, South Dakota, June 20, 1930.*

I am just coming into the very good hands of the Hutterian Smith Group. Michel Waldner, with his almost white hair and beard, is coming with his son Paul to fetch me. Now you can be quite at ease.

*June 24, 1930.*

The brothers and sisters are very, very loving to me and to all of you. . . . The spirit and reality of today's Hutterians surpass by far my, and our, expectations. The communication with God, the faith in the Holy Spirit and in Christ's redemption is alive here. Our great need in the Church for the Holy Spirit and His ever-renewed coming and acting and speaking is a very deep and strong awareness here. There is a loyalty to one another . . . in speaking, very good discipline is kept in not speaking about one another, but openly addressing one another. Joy and cheerfulness are constantly expressed in friendly humor with a depth of feeling and in even deeper words of faith from the Bible, from proverbs or experiences. The simplicity of the life is still kept fairly pure. For example, no Bruderhof buys a car, because they do not want to. Thus not only all the older brothers, but also many of the young people, men and women, have a deep joy and a full understanding of the flaring up of the fire of first love and beginning community with its special characteristics. . . . But what is hard for us to understand is the wealth of material goods and of the economy.

*Wolf Creek (Menno, South Dakota), July 2, 1930.* [Written for Eberhard by Elisabeth Hofer to Emmy Arnold.]

Dear Emma, I would like to write [dictate] more, but my eye is giving me pain.

*Wolf Creek, July 15, 1930.*

Today you will at last get a little letter from my hand

again. The eye doctor . . . who has been treating me for weeks, has not yet allowed reading and writing. But the eye now hurts only seldom and little. . . . This attack was the most painful and hardest to bear. Thursday I had to talk and tell a lot, until the pain became too bad. . . .

So through the illness much time has gone by. But I believe that these three weeks are not lost. From my bed . . . I experienced the daily life of the *Bruderhöfer*[4] in a special way and could without haste take up an inner attitude to everything that presses in upon me here. The faith of the Hutterians is real and genuine. It is rooted deeply in the hearts of all. They do not want to—they cannot—live any other way than in community. The practical forgetting of self in the service of the community is far stronger than with us. The seriousness of the divine witness to the truth is strong even with the simplest members. The calling to God is touching. How it moved me, when I was received as a guest to sleep in the room of the elderly Michel Waldner couple . . . , to see the old man praying in the dark room by his big chest in the wonderful dignity, reverence and supplication of the Hutterian (early Christian) attitude of prayer; on the knees, . . . hands held up to God before the face. The Brothers have no doubt that this is the attitude of the times of the apostles and the first baptisms: "Raise up the tired hands."—"Strengthen the tired knees!"

We in Germany have a very wrong concept of the lack of mission among the Brothers. To begin with, in spite of their extreme remoteness they are visited by unbelievable crowds of people, often by fifty cars on a single day. They admonish the people very clearly and firmly. However, in many individual talks with such guests, I became convinced

[4] Members of a Bruderhof.

that they have no questions, that they are not seekers. They come only on account of the world-wide fame that the Hutterians have. For example, I talked to a professor whom I met in Bon Homme as well as in Wolf Creek and who unfortunately wants to write still another book about the Hutterians, and I brought to his attention how many books he would have to read first. "Oh no," he said, "all that isn't necessary." Against such insolence the Brothers defend themselves hands and feet. . . . As soon as they realize that a man is not seeking the true life of God, they turn away and say, "He loves his own too much. He is not willing." . . . So my diary will tell a good deal more about the "non-mission." Yet—America lacks the *judgment of world war*, of revolution, of currency inflation; it lacks our movements of recent times. The social conscience is lacking. The feeling for God's Kingdom and His justice is lacking. One preaches to deaf ears. Here Mammon reigns undisputed, over the religious and the irreligious. . . . At the same time, however, the Brothers are aware that they are far from having true mission. . . . So they expect more from us than we have. For the power of faith is very great here. And everything is judged according to the Spirit—whether one speaks, lives, and works in the Spirit; whether one is loving and whether one speaks the truth openly. In short, it is life, true life from God with the witness of the new birth, so that the unanimity is astonishing. . . . The old Elder [David Hofer from Rockport] is in rather poor health. Recently he said, "If Arnold really comes from Germany and wants what they had in the old times, he will be very dissatisfied with us, if only because of our great possessions in land and money." He [David Hofer] is very much aggrieved about the development in Alberta. . . .

*Rockport, S.D., July 26.*

The task which I have to master here is too great to be able to accomplish it in a shortened time. You know that it is not my nature to be slow in regard to a duty once recognized, and especially toward a pressing need. And certainly my quickness to act has not always been a good thing!

*Lake Byron, S.D., August 5, 1930.* [In answer to my letter.]

What is this about holding back many things? W.'s name is also mentioned? I refrain from writing my opinion about this matter from a distance, and also about the matter of R. and I. It would look sharp. Rather I trust fully in you as brotherhood members ... not to overlook or neglect anything that destroys the community. ... How wonderful and important it must have been when you told about our engagement and uniting for Christ and our eventful way to the goal! You ought to ... write it down for me.

Yes, our Bruderhof is unbelievably rich in inner and outer experience. Today we cannot grasp the grace that is given to us in this. May we all make use of this unique opportunity to find true life.

And now the question of the confirmation of our service comes closer and closer. And how deeply and strongly the Hutterians understand this! ... When I think, not only of the twelve Articles of Faith (the apostolic Confession of Faith in the Hutterian sense), but also of Peter Rideman's momentous *Confession* and in addition of the discipline and order for the keeping pure and purification, for the unity and uniting of the brotherhood (as you have now experienced it anew), then I feel my weakness and sinfulness so very much that I would like most of all to see someone else from our circle in this position. But I dare not shirk it.

*Winnipeg, August 1930.*

Peter Hofer[5] says over and over again that the awakening, vitalizing and unifying of American Hutterdom would have to come through me. Only from us can he hope for it. And Joseph, the younger Kleinsasser, emphasizes—probably too much—that my visit and our "new zeal" has the greatest significance for them and that it occupies them a great deal and that they have been much stirred by it.... [About Joseph Kleinsasser the Elder:] In everything where we are really more radical and more Hutterian, he very clearly acknowledges that our beginning is right rather than his own people. But he is very much against any forcing, any trying to act in one's own strength. He is a man of faith, of the Spirit and of dependence on God.

*Winnipeg, August 25, 1930.*

The care for our Bruderhof "for the temporal need" is still very meager....

David Hofer of James Valley and Joseph Waldner of Huron, two of the most important representatives, represent the recognition that we have been tested and proven sufficiently by the fact of our continuing for several years and by the preservation of our orders and our basis, about which they are enthusiastic. They feel that therefore all that is necessary is to exchange with me the questions and answers required by order!... I mostly speak in free discussion before the gathered "people" until twelve midnight, sometimes until one o'clock, at least until ten or eleven o'clock. Here I receive the strongest impressions of the faith, love and firmness of the brothers and sisters, all of whom take part in the discussion ... and want to know in detail about you all and the children....

[5] Peter Hofer of James Valley, later Elder of the Smith Group.

*Winnipeg, September 4, 1930.*

I can't describe to you the deep joy that takes hold of me when I immerse myself again and again in your letters which have so much depth. . . . If only I could answer everything! I don't mean the unavoidable difficulties. For I don't want to go into these by letter at all, if possible, . . . and in the second place because God is so evidently giving you the help and strength to overcome everything. . . . [Here follows much about the debt burden of the Smith communities.]

In contrast to Germany, here the old people are mostly much more spirited and lively than the young people, who only begin at baptism on the long way toward attaining the same depth of faith.

In Manitoba I find my very best impressions of South Dakota confirmed, though the fears regarding a threatening decline, such as the all-too-old David Hofer of Rockport especially represents, are not without foundation. The young people are the problem, in Manitoba more than in South Dakota. But the abundant love and gratitude with which I am welcomed here is proof of the will, the longing, the faith, and pulsating life. I am often brought into great embarrassment when people say to me here on several Höfe that I should become the head man for all Bruderhöfe, so as to draw them together in the manner and strength of the early Hutterians and to lead them in the mission task. I know only too well that someone different from me would be needed for this.

Today, however, I don't want to tell so much about Manitoba, but rather go into your letters, which, like the others from our brothers and sisters, have made quite a powerful impression here on the Bruderhöfer, so that they simply can't hear and marvel enough. They all say, "You ask for mission, but your Hof with its guests is mission." There is much in this remark which we perhaps won't understand until later, some day when the flood of guests may be over. The Hutterian mission differs from evangelization by lecture and sermon in that it seeks out the "zealous"—and these only—in every place, challenges and gathers them and calls them home. . . . David Hofer of Rockport said, "If the Church is right, then there *will be* mission, if *not*, there will be *no* mission." . . . All brothers think unanimously that we should stay over there [Germany] as long as the "zeal" keeps up and as long as the school laws and authorities are not against us. . . .

Your prayers! I hope to come home healthier than I have ever been. Then all your worries . . . should be taken away.

I can just say to summarize that even the Hutterians of today are so completely unique in their almost perfect brotherly communal life, their objectivity, simplicity and fearless modesty that in Europe, as far as we know, there is nothing even approaching it. . . . All our expectations of faith coming from the "Christian Fellowship" movement, as well as from that of the youth movement and the religious-social movement, can be fulfilled here, even though certain signs of weakness, as in everything human, are unmistakable.

*Cardston (Alberta), October 2, 1930.*

The fact that such quite old men have the leadership has the advantage that it assures to a high degree the holding on to what is old and proven, to the genuine and original Hutterianism. This advantage surely removes the disadvantage of less flexibility and receptivity, which is to be felt in spite of all alertness and liveliness. . . . And today is the

2nd of October, the day when in the year 1899 I had the first fully conscious experience and encounter with our Savior and Redeemer Jesus Christ. At that time you, too, already had deep impressions of Him, our beloved Jesus, in your childhood, and gave yourself fully to Him. I am confident that the uniting with the Hutterians will bring to you and me and all of us . . . the complete fulfillment of our longing in faith for so many years. . . .

*Lethbridge (Alberta), October 8, 1930.*

Now begins the time you foretold to me. I would not be able to bear too long the separation from you, from our children, from our home, from our dear, faithful Bruder-höfer and our so characteristic and unique community of life. But I must be firm and hold out. Here too the Hutterians are very loving, attentive, interested and have very warm and awakened hearts for our cause. And yet it is harder than I can say that still—until today!—I can speak only very seldom of the pressing need of our financial situation, a need which is unknown here. All have the opinion, with the well-known rigid firmness of Hutterdom, that the spiritual things must be regulated first, and only then the temporal. . . . Wherever I can do so without hurting our cause, I speak of $25,000 which I want to bring home at Christmas. Hutterian naiveté asks in reply with earnest eyes, "So much at once?"

*Lethbridge, October 23, 1930.*

You will be worried by now. And in fact it was the eye again. . . . It cost a week and $35. Now I want to go through the Bruderhöfe again, more slowly this time. When I go too fast, especially when I have to share the bed with Andreas *Vetter* of Old Elm Spring, it immediately throws the strain onto the eye. . . . At the same time I am pursued and overwhelmed all too much by love. And I am getting fearful that they will set much too "high" expectations on me. I believe the wealth of old writings being presented to us is very promising for help in other respects, which is to surprise us.

*Millford, October-November.*

Today I shall go with the Servant of the Word and Steward of Buck Ranch, Millford, to Johann Wurz at Richards *Gemein* ["community"] near Wilson. We are to go in a closed car because of my eyes, since the trips in open wagons with a lively wind did them no good. . . . You can imagine that with such enthusiasm, especially as the brothers and sisters of the Bruderhöfe all come thronging to me, I don't have a minute of rest. This is not a complaint. As Johannes Wurz says, we should thank God with all our hearts that such a great awakening has come about through my visit, from which very many, though not all, expect renewal, uniting and mission! . . . The worst part of it is, however, that the date of my departure has been put in question by the urgent requests of our faithful Elias Walter. Please don't do anything to hinder this. Every fiber in me is urging me homewards. But the goal of this costly and strenuous journey must not be endangered by our impatience and longing. . . .

*Lethbridge, November 12, 1930.*

There is a good prospect that we can set up our Hof. . . . But it is not achieved yet.

*Crow's Nest, British Columbia, November 30.*

I can hardly endure it anymore to be separated from you so long, . . . and not least, being so far from the beloved circle of our old and new faithful co-fighters—yes, from the whole unique spirit and life of our Bruderhof. . . . On practically all Bruderhöfe the meetings were wonderful, with their many hours of uninterrupted attentiveness and enthusiasm and thankfulness. I am so ardently sought after that neither in Lethbridge nor in Macleod, Cardston, or Calgary, or even in smaller places have I found as much as half a day's rest for writing, without being sought out and fetched away. . . . And all community members, thus not only ours, are easily hurt if a "guest from so far away and one living in real community" has no time at all for an important inner and brotherly talk! So, just as at the time of our engagement (which I am asked to tell about again and again), I have fled to the mountains so as to write you at least a short letter. . . .

The more firmly all at home stand together, the more secure I can be here — and come home with great new help!

*Rocky Mountains, November 26, 1930.*

To the whole Sun Troop and to all the little and smallest children, whom I love so dearly, I must write another time that you should not be surprised by your ups and downs. For you are small human beings, and you will have to accept and become reconciled to the fact that human nature needs many who are guided and led and a few who have the strength to lead, but who again from their innermost hearts cry out for guidance.

You should desire the innermost freedom in the agreement of hearts, but not too much independence in the expression of opinions. The good, pure Spirit will continue, as in the past, to be your true and ultimately only Leader, but not without weak, human tools, who have to transmit His guidance!

This goes just as much for us adults! And here I come

to the factual content of my letter. How happy, how glad
and joyful I am about the clear guidance through the Holy
Spirit which you have been given during all these months,
and indeed again and again through the tools appointed by
God and His Church. And with what faithfulness you have
stood to the Brothers and the communities that are called
Hutterites, because Jakob Hutter founded them with the
glowing, burning fire of love and with equally glowing and
fiery discipline. In the same way you have stood to their
deeply tested orders, almost without the slightest inter-
ruption, which would have been all too understandable
humanly. I can limit myself to a few brief sentences of
reminder in this second, objective part. For you have been
crowned by the Spirit Himself, far better than all the old
priests and rulers!

And now you have a veritable treasure of writings that
radiate the Spirit, already more than 150 handwritten books,
"little books," pamphlets and leaflets, among them more
than fifty old and very old pieces; only very few of the
American Bruderhöfe have such a precious treasure of
old handwritings. So great is the love of the Brothers to
us that they will surely not let us down on the economic
side. However, with their persistent thoroughness all this
will take time, much time; and so with a heavy heart I must
again ask you for leave of absence, even with my poor health
and my bad eye, which varies but has never again been as
bad as it was at home in the spring, during the journey and
in June in Wolf Creek. Be assured that I shall come home
as fast as possible, as soon as my task of finding unity,
support for the service and for the economic basis of our
Bruderhof, has been solved to a certain degree. Since I
feel now each time how much the stream of energy and

power is weakened and diverted that comes to me from your unity in truth, in prayer, in the breaking of bread and in the community, I ask you in deep and heartfelt trust: Do not urge me to return too soon, for this might put into question the whole success of these great sacrifices.

Trust in your leading, that it will guide you through everything in unity through God's Spirit. Be openhearted, open and ready for one another! Have joy in one another! You have much cause for this! Together with your openness and your youthfulness in God, preserve your fine feeling for the purity and unity in the Spirit. But become free and remain free from personal touchiness, from worry about being treated differently from others, also in your tasks, duties and services! For there is really no cause for this!

Rejoice in your spiritual unity and in your real standing together, even in your diversity, without trying to make equal, align, level and paralyze—and thus to dissolve and extinguish—all special qualities. Community lives only in living reciprocity! Therefore rejoice in your diversity and never be offended by it!

But with all this diversity of typical, characteristic and varied gifts and talents, there are things that can never be allowed—selfishness and pettiness, talking behind others' backs, envy and jealousy, fear and worry and worse things. Like self-seeking and self-will, these enemies of life are not gifts of the Spirit, but sheer loss and damage. There is no one who has received so few gifts that he has to make a good-for-nothing of himself through his concern with these dangerous trivialities! Such poison and nothingness is beneath us! Please, yes, I plead with you, persevere for yet a short while all together, in full unity and divine love and joy. Don't waste a single night on things, questions and discussions which would be unnecessary if we stood together more faithfully, more firmly, more trustingly and more gratefully. In other words, make such nights unnecessary by not letting anything come to pass that would make them necessary.

Please—yes, I earnestly ask you: Carry your great and holy responsibility steadfastly, like a burning light in your hands. For the sake of this warming, radiating light, do not let yourselves be pushed or shaken or even knocked over! Then the fullness of your burning candles will send its light over to me as in a Christmas vision and will strengthen me and bring me back with everything you need. You know that the incarnation of the Creator and His word of love, and Jesus' word and work in the outpouring of His Spirit, is the strength in which you can do everything.

Therefore let no strange, dark, unclear or apathetic spirit enter among you or rule over you, not even through your guests, relatives, visitors, or old and new friends. . . .Let nothing, not the slightest thing, come among you that offends Jesus Christ, His world redemption, His smallness and humbleness and redemption in the manger and on the Cross, His following on His way to men and to God, His obedience to the words of His Sermon on the Mount, His now truly outpoured Spirit of full unity and purity and active reality.

The Lord is the Spirit. Only in the Spirit of unity shall we see the Christ of purity. Only thus shall we come to faith in the all-powerful Creator, God of all worlds and suns and earths, who in Christ and in the outpoured Spirit of His Church has become our Father, to whom we belong and whom we trust that He will provide us with everything we need. . . .

*Stand Off Bruderhof (Macleod, Alberta), with Elias Walter, December 1, 1930.*

For the next two weeks, as for the last weeks, I am especially heavily engaged by Elias Walter; accompanied by him with great love, I am traveling through the last northerly Church-communities. . . . Since my eye, though not bad, is also still not quite well, I try as often as possible to go in a closed car when there is a sharp wind. . . .

*Lethbridge, for Christmas and your birthday.*

I would never, never have thought that I . . . would have to write to you from this great distance! But the view is becoming clearer. And I already see clearly that this hard renunciation leads to the goal . . . also my eye illness was used by God, who guides *everything* so that the brothers in America will finally open their too-careful hearts unreservedly to the cause entrusted to us in Germany, . . . as Elias Walter has done for many years now. So today I write to you for your dear Christmas-birthday as . . . a real Hutterian brother. For the fact that I have been taken in as a brother would mean that we would also be taken care of as brothers. And the time of alms would be past; now establishment and mission would begin. . . . God the true One has ordained it in such a way that they were all unanimous to accept me and incorporate me on December 9, 1930. I will write you in detail about this as soon as the confirmation of my Service of the Word for the mission and establishment of our Bruderhof has taken place on December 17; all Servants of the Word in America are invited to this. On account of the injection [for eye trouble] I cannot write more today. . . . May God in His indescribable mercy grant that we meet again soon and with a truly successful result for our Bruderhof!

To the Housemother, the Steward and the Brotherhood, Christmas 1930. The support and arrangement is planned as follows:

1) Debt-free Bruderhöfe, $1000 each
2) Half-indebted Bruderhöfe, $500 each
   (completely indebted Bruderhöfe, nothing)
3) Thirty high grade work horses to be sent over the sea for our Bruderhof and for selling.
4) Likewise fifteen high grade milch cows. . . .

*Stand Off, December 25 and 31, 1930.*

There is no other course for me than to travel once more through the Bruderhöfe of Alberta now in order to gather the brothers everywhere and to ask for a really large sum. It will be very strenuous for me . . . , there is not a free minute from early morning until late in the evening. And my nervous system and my body, and perhaps also my inner life, is not really adjusted to this, so that after several days of this I am always quite exhausted. . . . I must pull together all my strength to carry on with raising funds for our expansion.

Just for this reason I tried by means of the seven-fold injection to make sure about my eye, which is still quite bad, so as to be able to cope with the fatigue of still one more round trip through Alberta. . . . There is only one possibility of storming these fortresses, and that is to besiege them continuously, like the widow, persistently. . . . The old Christian *Vetter*,[6] who presided at the big confirmation meeting of the twenty-one Servants, in this meeting was very unwilling to give more extensive support, especially as his Raley Bruderhof has used up its funds completely through a large purchase of land. . . .

[6] Elder of the Darius Group.

Whenever I was not so well, I usually did not write to you at all and waited until my eye and health were better and stronger. But this time the fever-cure for the eye and the overstrain from the communal work and the traveling followed so quickly one after the other that I cannot let you, and all of you, go longer without news of me. . . . At the same time I have much cause for joy here too. But I believe that this joy will not break through completely until I am at home with you again and can rejoice with you and all the brothers and sisters in the support for our community and our Bruderhof, which is after all the best.

*Calgary, Canada, January 20, 1931.*

I am longing to be able to do the joyful work of building up, both inward and outward, after I return home, without being hindered too much, as we were before, by the debts which burdened our conscience.

I could report many wonderful things about the powerful religious awakening in a number of communities . . . not only women, but strong men, shed tears and want to hear more and more.

*Lethbridge, February 1931.*

Just a short greeting from my strenuous fund-raising journey, which is having a gradual and still only partially satisfactory success. I was again on twelve Höfe for this. . . . And our beloved Bruderhof! It is and remains for us the best, the only possible one. I have been deeply confirmed in this here, also that we should stay as long as at all possible in the German land in Europe, which again is suffering and struggling so heavily.

*Lethbridge, February 1931.*

Everything urges me to hurry to you, but my money-

raising was interrupted ... so that I again turned to the
work with the books (the writings I have now sent). But
now it goes forward again.... The raising of money brings
slow results—though it does bring some results—so that
one would have to give up hope of attaining such a large
amount (needed for our building up) if a higher faith did
not guide us, making us independent of circumstances. So
I must still persist.... The impressions here confirm my
awareness of how necessary it is for the life in community
to have properly trained people.

*Lethbridge, March 1931.*
　Also those [piano] lessons with Trautel (to whom I send
my special greetings) ... cannot be "forbidden" any more
than any other basic training. What we are concerned with
here is a question of religious usage or tradition; that is,
that no idolatry, including that of musical feeling, should
crowd out the faith in the Spirit.

*Lethbridge, March 1931.*
　Now the departure is finally here. There is my worn-out
first suit ... then two Hutterian hats for our museum. Also to
be saved for the museum, not to be used, is the broom of
the Hutterian workshop from Jakob at Old Elm Spring,
more than 70 years old, made and presented by him.

*South Dakota, April 10, 1931.*
　This unique opportunity must be utilized! I certainly
know that I will never again in my life undertake such a
journey alone, without you! Even though I have gained a
lot of weight and found the best of care and most loving
reception everywhere, still the homesickness and the distance
from the unique freshness of spirit at Sannerz and the Rhön
Bruderhof was so very hard.... How marvelously has the

good and strong Spirit of God and Jesus Christ, the enliven-
ing and purifying Spirit of community, held us—except for
Hugga—together! What grace!

We must be courageous! You ask about the reasons for
the . . . prolongation of the journey. They consist, 1) in me:
in the eye illness and poor health, 2) in the indescribable
difficulties of asking for money, 3) in the handwritten
manuscripts, etc. . . . Only my telling it all in person will
make everything understandable.

*Radio-telegram, May 1, 1931.*

On ocean at last. Meet me Bremerhaven Sunday May 10.
Happy your Eberhard.

Now, how did things go otherwise during Eberhard's trip
to America? Seen as a whole, it went really very well. It had
been given over to Hans, then twenty-three years old, to
represent Eberhard; those who did the other services—housemother, steward, work distributor and storekeeper—tried to
stand by him in a special way in the daily life. Of course, the
whole brotherhood supported him! The life was not without
struggles. Ambition and arrogance, the perpetual enemies of
the community life, came to the fore soon after Eberhard's
departure. Again and again we had to occupy ourselves with
our own and others' weaknesses. But it was good that these
things were repeatedly taken in hand and overcome by the
entire brotherhood. It was given to Hans at that time to see
the way and the direction and to hold to it in a very loving
but clear way.

In the summer we had many guests; once we had a work
camp with Erich Mohr's Free German Work League. The
work campers, together with our brothers, were to drain a
wet, sour meadow. For this, long ditches were laid out. In the

discussions with these work campers, vegetarianism played a special role. This conference or work-community did not lead to particular experiences. Letters written by myself and others at this time still exist.

We were extremely short of money, and it was hard to steer the way through. From time to time sums of money came from North America as Eberhard was able to send them, and these were a help in stopping different gaps. Eberhard's letters, which were sent to me in particular, were received with the greatest interest and read in the brotherhood meetings. It was a great disappointment for us that his return did not take place before Christmas, as we had hoped, but only in May. On our wedding anniversary, December 20, however, came the news via cable that the uniting with the Brothers—with all three groups, that is, the Teacher (*Lehrer*), Darius (*Darius*) and Smith (*Schmiede*) Groups—had taken place at the Stand Off community, Elias Walter's Bruderhof! There was great rejoicing, and the return now seemed to us to be very close. But the next news was another disappointment for us; it was that Eberhard was to travel to all Bruderhöfe once more in order to get help for our new beginning. And this again in an open wagon in the [Canadian] winter and early spring, with his eye trouble which had already several times cost him so much time and strength.

To his great joy, a large number of very old handwritten manuscripts were presented to him. For one thing, there were no longer many among the Hutterians who were able to read this old German handwriting; and besides, they were not read much anymore in any case, because this ancient, pithy language no longer spoke to the Hutterians of today. They were more receptive to the later teachings which came from a less powerful time, for these were better suited to their life. The earlier writings no longer seemed to them suitable for the times in which they were living. We, on the contrary, in fact felt spoken to only by this beginning time of Hutterianism—by Jakob Hutter, Ulrich Stadler and others.

On Eberhard's return, we were disappointed in the results of his strenuous efforts over a whole year to get financial help; for these results were small, considering the circumstances of the Hutterians. From about forty Hutterian communities very little was raised toward the building up or toward paying off debts for our beginning group which had to struggle under such difficult conditions following a great World War. Thus the slow and laborious work of building up continued.

# BETWEEN TIME AND ETERNITY

EBERHARD'S RETURN on May 10, 1931, for which we had waited so long, was a very great joy and strengthening. It was May 1 when we received the telegram from on board the ship *Berlin* saying that he would arrive in Bremerhaven on the morning of May 10. We talked it over and it was decided in the brotherhood that Hans and I should go there to fetch him. Our Tata (Else) was unfortunately not there. Through the kindness of Friedrich Wilhelm Förster, she was enabled to go to Switzerland and there, in the mountain air, to gain health and strength in the convalescent home of a friend, Maria Arbenz, since she was suffering from tuberculosis of the lungs. It was expected that her tasks as secretary would increase more and more after Eberhard's return, especially in the work with the old books and writings. She stayed in Switzerland until July. Emi-Ma had passed her exams as kindergarten teacher, in Thale in the Harz Mountains, in the autumn of 1930, and Hardi had graduated at Easter from the Hermann Lietz country boarding school in Bieberstein. Both were now brotherhood members and could take an active part in the building up. Hardi, having been away for three years, was now to help in the farm work for a year before beginning his university studies.

Hans and I, then, went to Bremen and on to Bremerhaven on May 9, since the ship was expected as early as six o'clock the next morning. So punctually we stood at the dock and watched the ship approach from a distance. We saw many people on the deck waving to their relatives. But we could not see Eberhard, until finally we discovered him standing at the end of the ship. What a reunion that was after one year's absence! We had so much to tell each other, first with Hans, and then also alone. There was so much that we had experienced at home.

Eberhard had received much love from the Brothers, but in spite of all his efforts, the financial success was small. Well, we were happy and glad that Eberhard was back again and that now he could once more discuss the future and the building up with us and advise us. We had by no means lost courage and faith.

In one of the first brotherhood meetings after this, it was decided that the four engaged couples were to be married. They were Leo and Trautel, Alfred and Gretel, Hans and and Emi-Ma, Walter and Trudi. So we planned to prepare four rooms for these, the first couples of 1931. For many others, too, we had to make room. Not all of the money from the American journey was still at our disposal, since a considerable part of it had come during the year to cover debts and was already spent. Other creditors had been put off until Eberhard's return. Thus no larger funds were available.

The first two weddings took place at the time of the summer solstice; that of Hans and Emi-Ma was on July 26, Eberhard's forty-eighth birthday. All the weddings were prepared with great love and great joy. We made the furniture ourselves, all in the same plain, simple style, but stained variously in red, brown and dark stains. The rooms were painted in plain bright colors—orange, yellow, light green. Each couple received two beds, a table, a corner bench, two chairs and a washstand. Simple bright curtains hung at the windows. Everything looked so harmonious, pretty and colorful.

Hans and Emi-Ma's wedding was crowned by the fact that our dear Tata returned from Switzerland. She was no longer to work full-time, although almost till the last hour of her life she continued to be occupied whenever possible, first working at the typewriter on minutes and letters, and later either on her long chair out in the open air, or during the last time in bed in her little hut which was especially fixed up for her.

Although the help expected from the journey to America had not come, the year 1931–1932 became the greatest year of growth we had had up to that time, through additional families coming to us from Switzerland, in particular the Boller family. These families brought with them the money we needed, almost exactly the amount we had hoped for from America. Thus it came to us from a quite unexpected source.

The work of preparation went ahead feverishly; sometimes building was going on in three places at once. Two new houses were built, a pigsty, a horse stable, a bakery; workshops were set up. All the money that came in was used for purposes of building up; no money was to be left lying in the bank. Now again there was a joyous spirit of building up. Guests came, helpers turned up, single young men and young girls. Annemarie Wächter (later Arnold) and our dear Ria Kiefer were among those who came as guests at this time. Nils and Dora came from Sweden not long after Eberhard's return. They were married at the Rhön Bruderhof in the autumn of 1932. Friedel S. had arrived during Eberhard's time in America. He also stayed to join us.

Each day brought new joy and new courage. All our work and efforts went into setting up a true, ordered Bruderhof, in contrast to the years when so much time and strength had to be used to obtain the means for building up and then to extend loans by many trips near and far. Many guests came with all their personal questions and concepts of life. Sick people came, including some with mental illness, seeking help. Individual cases are difficult to report; some victories were won and there were also some defeats. Hutterianism and some things in it which had not grown in the same way with us were also important questions for us. Other things that were much discussed were the nationalistic world view, vegetarianism, marriage and family, and so on. How stimulating and exciting were many of these evenings under the great beech at the edge of the *Küppel* (knoll) on the side toward Gundhelm. Many of these guest meetings were taken down in shorthand and are to be found in our archives. I have put together and copied two volumes of such records of meetings.

When the discussions were particularly moving, Eberhard forgot time completely, just as in the early years of our life together. So the midday or evening meal often went on for a very long time if a good discussion with guests developed. This sometimes made it difficult in the work, especially as Eberhard did not like it if anyone stayed away washing the dishes or doing anything else. *Everybody* had to join in the experience; they were all called in! Thus he never announced at the mealtime what further meeting was planned for the evening, so that no one would feel left out. Sometimes it took quite a while until one or the other left with a guest or guests for a walk or to show them the brotherhood room or the new children's house. Occasionally it would happen that later on a guest came in again during a *Gemeindestunde* (inner meeting) or brotherhood meeting. Eberhard could quickly change the subject and turn toward the guest. Of course this gift often caused delays in the work that had to be done.

Each person felt that the communal experience had a special worth. The daily work was done together quickly and joyfully. In these years the work of building up was done with the same great joy as in the beginning of our life in community. The difference was that now there was money, whereas at that time we were forced to build up without capital. So often Eberhard said, "God has blessed us in that we did not want to establish our *own* work." For example, he meant our joining the old Hutterian movement. If the means do not come through *our* methods, God has quite different ways. And so it was that these means came to us through new members joining us.

It was midsummer already, and much needed to be done before winter set in, to accommodate the newcomers. First of all came the Boller family, who wanted to unite with us completely when they had settled their connections with the Church authorities and wound up their financial affairs. They belonged to the religious-social group in Switzerland. They had been present at the wedding of Hans and Emi-Ma in July 1931, and felt very much challenged by this experience. After they had expressed the wish to come to live with us rather than to join the *Werkhof* near Zurich, we had long discussions with them every evening about the basis of our life. We talked about the Church, education, property, the State and many other things. These talks led to their wishing to break off everything in order to be able to come to us as quickly as possible. Before going back to do this early in August they entered the novitiate, and after arranging everything, they came to us with their children in October.

What a joyful arrival this was—our first family from Switzerland! Other Swiss families soon followed, the Mathis' in 1932 and the Meiers early in 1933. There were also other

Swiss who came to us. Trautel Fischli and Walter Hüssy had already come in 1929, and others followed — Lini Rudolph, Margot Salvodelli, Julia Lerchy and others, quite a group of Swiss, who helped us a great deal in the building up.

Even in the midst of this joyful time we also had some difficult experiences, some frightening. Because of the urgency of the building, which was going on in three places at once, we had to employ workers from the neighborhood. We never needed larger sums of money on the Bruderhof itself, and so incoming money was deposited in our bank in Fulda. Every Friday, before the workers' payday, someone would go in to Fulda to get the money to pay them. On one certain Friday, Hans and Arno were the ones who went in. It was one of those foggy October or November days when they came driving along in our buggy. On the way home, they had just reached the top of the hill toward Eichenried when their wagon was suddenly stopped, and two or three masked men stood before them holding pistols to their chests and saying, "Give us your money, or we'll shoot!" They did not give the money over. Hans stood with arms crossed across his chest, thereby holding onto the wallet containing the money — more than 500 marks. The men then forcibly seized the wallet with its contents and ran off, the one saying to the other, "Let them live!"

The rest of us, not having any idea of what was happening, were sitting in the brotherhood room. Suddenly Arno burst in, very excited, and told us all about what had happened. Once the first dismay had passed, how thankful we were that the two brothers were safe and well among us. And we were thankful, too, that they had not voluntarily handed over the money, which belonged to the Church!

The District Administrator, von Gagern, who wrote us a letter in memory of Eberhard on the occasion of Eberhard's

seventieth birthday anniversary, mentioned this assault in his
letter. He wrote:

> I have often admired the consistency of the Bruderhof
> members in their Christian attitude to life. For example,
> two of them who were carrying the week's pay for their
> workers—one of them a giant with the strength of a
> bear—were attacked in the wood by masked figures. Re-
> membering the words of the Savior, they did not defend
> themselves, but allowed themselves to be robbed.

We did not inform the police about this attack, of course. We
did, however, invite the neighbors and especially the workers
who were helping us in the building work to a meeting and
told them about the occurrence. We asked them, in case they
should ever find out anything about it, to see that the money,
which belonged not to us but to the cause, was returned. We
never heard any more about it.

This same night was the first bad night for our Tata, who
was already then pretty much confined to her bed. We told
her nothing about the event, although someone did sleep with
her. But in the little hut where she lay, she had an uneasy
feeling that something had happened. Not until the morning,
while Karl was heating her stove, did she hear the story from
him with all details.

From that time on, Tata's health went downhill. There are
a number of reports about that time until her death that can
tell about it better than I can do after more than thirty years.
There is an address spoken in the brotherhood the morning of
her burial, and another spoken probably on the day of Tata's
death or the day after. And yet the details and the witness
of eternity still live quite strongly in my memory. Thus one
feels the strong bond with those who have gone on before.

She was one of those first ones who began our life in community, and she was loved by old and young. There was something of Francis of Assisi in her; in spite of all the work and her devotion to it, she always had time for the needs of her fellowmen. Her trips in the near neighborhood and farther afield to beg for help were not without results. Who could resist this person, so enthusiastic but so poor in body?

Of our Else von Hollander, of the faith that lived in her, Eberhard wrote after her death in a printed circular letter to friends:

> The death of Jesus Christ, and with Him the death of the old martyrs, was constantly before the eyes of our Else as she was dying, so that she had to testify, "Nothing greater can happen than the death of Christ. It is the greatest thing, and just in this God's mercy shows itself, mercy in judgment." Because of this the dying woman was so deeply gripped by the longing for Jesus and for the Kingdom of Heaven that she said over and over again, "The Spirit and the Bride speak: Come, amen, yes come, Lord Jesus. — The powers of Eternity are very near. I am just as weak a person as ever; that has not changed at all. But Christ's nearness is much stronger than ever. Because of this I am quite far away from [temporal] events here. I am quite close to what is happening there [in Heaven]. And yet I am very close to the happenings here [God's present temporal history]; but it is as if I were looking on at them from another star. For myself I cannot think or wish for anything earthly."

> One of her last words was, "Lift me up and let me hold my head up."

> On January 1 she said, "The year 1932 will be a very special year, a year of great struggles and of great building up. But there is no life here without struggle; the new life must come through death. . . . "

She said, "Though I need help now, we shall all experience Eternity then. Eternity! That is something one can't understand; one can't grasp it. Eternity has always been. And Eternity will always be. And I need so much to feel Eternity now. Eternity is very close to me, and its powers are coming to me. It is God. That which is greatest in God is mercy. That is so wonderful. And it is so wonderful to live in brotherhood. The love and faithfulness of our brotherhood is a miracle. It is quite unbelievable that this is possible. How much I love them all! And how dear they all are. For the young people a strengthening in the mental and spiritual must come; in struggle and strife against themselves, in steady work, they must become free of all unclearness and all touchy feelings. I see clearly that the Bruderhof will become very big, and I am very glad that I was allowed to be part of the small beginning of the building up. The influence upon the whole world will become great, also in the mission outside. I shall experience this with you from Eternity and shall surely be able to help a little too. Whenever the Spirit of the Church unites you fully and strengthens you for the work, I too will be there; for in the Holy Spirit the whole Church of the Spirit is amongst you. The Holy Spirit brings the complete Church of the Jerusalem above down to you.

"I am so thankful for the unity. The unity in the Spirit and in the things of the Spirit—this is what endures. All that we do could be the expression of unity; but that is only the expression. Unity itself is different and greater than all outward expression. That is so wonderful—all unity that is to endure must be built only on the Spirit. The expression perishes, but the unity endures.

"It is so wonderful to adore God. I should like to

adore Him always. God is so good, so good. Eternal life is so close to me, much closer than anything else." She looked toward the window and asked, "Are the stars shining now? That is where I shall be brought to. I would like so much to be with the prophets, the apostles, and martyrs, but probably I shall first be only with the little children. I have only one request, that Christ come to get me Himself. He is always very close to me now. Sometimes I would like to ask God to be able to go to sleep dreaming and without the pains of death, and wake up in Eternity. But that would be too impudent."

In the midst of the worst pain and torment she could cry, "It is so wonderful, I am so glad, and here in the Church it is so wonderful. The life in the brotherhood is something wonderful. How I rejoice in the building up. A great time is coming in this year, but it will come through struggle and strife. When things become difficult, you must always hold to the faith. You must always think then, God is the Victor in the end. Life is struggle and strife; in death this struggle becomes strongest. In life people often don't notice this struggle at all, and therefore they don't take it seriously enough. At the end the struggle is worst and hardest. The last half year has strengthened us very much in the faith that God is with us. Though we become weak again and again, we are always allowed to have faith that God will concern Himself with us in our weakness."

Another time she told our children, "I am thinking about the ship on which Papa went to America. He wrote then, 'Let us pray that it will be a good landing in the right land of God.' And here is our Rhön land where our Bruderhof is; here I shall embark and travel to another

Land, to the most beautiful Land. I see a great procession full of light. They are all there, all, and they call to me, 'Come with us!' But Christ is not at their head or behind them; He is with me. I have fought a great fight."

Once when she was looking out of the window from her bed with wide, expectant eyes, she was asked, "Do you see someone?" She answered, "No. But I must always watch to see when it is coming. Over and over I experience the Revelation of John: The Spirit and the Bride say, 'Come!' "

Often she would turn away and look off in the distance and say several times, quite softly, "Lord, come soon!—It is so beautiful to see the morning dawning; how will it be, then, when the Eternal Morning begins."

During the night she sometimes awakened, opened her eyes wide with a clear look and placed her raised hands together in prayer. And once she said, "My spirit is already far away, but also completely with all of you. I have a foretaste of Eternity. I feel as though I were standing between time and Eternity, as though I were connecting you with Eternity. I need Jesus much more than ever; if only He would come soon to get me. Mercy is the doorway. The greatest thing in God is mercy. I am so happy about the complete unity. That is the main thing. God is Bond, God is Covenant. If I am to depart some day, do not part from me! Now sing and be joyful. . . . "

During the last days she recalled how she had seen a remarkable vision of light. Down on earth she had seen a great, powerful, smoky fire that was not clear or bright, and she had felt an oppressive fear that this fire could destroy everything. But then in the middle of this dark red, smoky fire a tiny, pure white flame, very clear and pure, had broken out, and this pure, white little flame had been her comfort. Then she had seen how this small flame spread out more and more. Then there came from above a very great, pure, bright flame of light which came down from Heaven and united with the small white flame. As soon as this had happened, a great city was formed out of this pure light. The smoky, sooty fire receded further and further back. Finally the city of light had become so extremely bright that the beginning and the walls of the city could no longer be seen. It had become all sun—one single, great, completely white and pure light. This experience of her faith was the shining forth of faith in the Church and the coming down of the Spirit upon the Church for the building of the city on the hill. In this sense she said about the reception of new members into our Church-community, "It is the community of the Eternal."

For me personally her death meant a real farewell out of my life, for had she not been my playmate and companion, from childhood on, in a special way? And in our period of awakening and time of engagement in 1907, she was one of our best helpers and co-fighters. One year after her death I wrote these lines, dated January 8, 1933:

Often it seems to me you must come in,
You who bore everything with us.
We awaited you often and went to meet you
As you returned from trips so difficult
Which you undertook, the task entrusted to you.
Sometimes the present is like a dream to me,
For I live in the past as much as in the future.
So clearly I see you before me
When we both were still children

And shared together joy and sorrow.
Then our father would say to us,
"Surely you two are thinking up nonsense again
When you put your heads together so quietly
And whisper to each other!"
We shared everything together,
Also our seeking and asking for the things of God.
And when the hour of decision, of calling, struck for me,
You too followed soon and left home,
To the pain and sorrow of our parents.
I then went with the one whom God allotted me as life-
      companion,
And on our wedding day—one of the high points in my
      life—
Your heart was divided between joy and grief,
For the companion of your childhood and youth
Was destined for marriage by God's innermost leading.
Yet soon God called you too to walk in company with us;
By divine direction tasks were set us
For which we urgently needed help.
So you worked together with us in Halle, Tyrol and Berlin,
Until the day when we were told
To leave everything and go into an unknown land!
Together with you and others, then, we were able
To begin the building up in Sannerz and the Rhön
      Bruderhof.
Those years of wrestling and struggling,
Of being opposed and defeated,
Of power and of victory,
Of walking on the level land
So near to the abyss,
Did not pass without leaving their mark on us!

To a special degree did you receive powers
Through God's assistance.
With your help the work was born,
And, never considering your health,
You consecrated your life to the highest service
Until the very last hour
Given you on this earth!
Like a ripe fruit from a tree, you fell.
Your life appears before our eyes as a completed whole,
For you were—yes, you are—fitted in,
As one stone next to others, in the Temple
Which is God's Building.
Although we know and believe
That you live and work, though dead to this time,
Why are one's feelings so earthly
That in thoughts one seeks you
In your work, your devotion, in the dress
You wore when here, still active among us!
How often am I sunk in thought
And feel that you must come back again,
And, waking and dreaming, look with longing for your
       return!
It is often a deep pain for me
That never again am I to see you as you were
Before you left us;
Your loyal face, your eyes warm with love.
When I pursued this thought,
Failing to understand what this separation means,
The answer came to me—from the other, the divine,
       world:
Why do you seek one who is living among the dead?
Eternity means fulfillment,
Fulfillment of life, of work, of time;

And the words of John again came to my remembrance:
There shall be no more sorrow and no separation,
For—the first life is over!
Thus we ask, united with you
Who have gone on before us:
Lord, come soon and establish Thy Kingdom
And unite all that is given to Thee
And what is fitted into the Body of Christ,
The Building of divine promise and destiny!
Here as well as there the Bride of the Lamb
Awaits the fulfillment of times and eternities—
The completion of the temple—
The new body, which is not consecrated to death
By separation from God,
But in the highest unity
Is destined for immortality.
Yes, Amen!

These reports, written at that time, say more than if I were
to write much about it today. Those last months that Else still
lived among us were a great challenge to us all. Often it seemed
as if she had already left us and come back again, because she
was able to tell us so much about the other life. One time on
awakening from a very deep sleep she said, "The life there
is much more lively than here; there is much more life!" She
also had visions for the life here, that the message of discipleship in the Church would be spread afar, as for example the
vision of the small white flame in the midst of a cloudy, sooty
atmosphere, which persisted more and more until it finally
united with the light of the Church from above and spread
out farther and farther until at last there was nothing but
light on the earth and in the whole universe! The world of
the stars was very close to her.

In a talk where she was asked what she would wish, she said, "I would *only* like to have more love!" She did not ask for more days or for a shortening of her severe physical suffering, but for more love.

In between she went on working with Eberhard, especially on the old writings and on meeting reports. She also took part in everything that went on in the brotherhood, in the household, anywhere in the world. She was very interested in the building up and also in the guests, and the children had a special relationship with her.

On her last birthday, shortly before Christmas, the wedding of Walter and Trudi took place. The whole time of Christmas and afterwards until her death on January 11 was dominated by our experience of her last days and all that she had to say to us. On January 11, after a night during which she had frequent attacks of choking, we were gathered around her bed. When she had drawn her last, difficult breaths, we could only sing, "Now thank we all our God!" She had conquered. She was probably conscious until the last moment.

## BEFORE THE STORM

LIFE WENT ON. It would not have been Else's wish to hold us up in anything. She had asked us not to stop the preparations for the coming double wedding on her account. The wedding of the two couples, Fritz Kleiner and Martha Sekunda Braun, and Arno Martin and our adopted Ruth von Hollander, took place on January 23 and 24, twelve days after the death of Else, in a truly gathered and united spirit.

In March, Eberhard and Adolf Braun went to a Religious Socialist conference in Bad Boll in Württemberg. This was the place where Johann Christoph Blumhardt and his son, Christoph Blumhardt, had worked for over seventy years for God's Kingdom. Eberhard reported about his impressions of Bad Boll in a meeting at the Rhön Bruderhof on April 3, 1932, as follows:

I want to try to summarize what various friends of Christoph Blumhardt told us, as we heard it in Bad Boll, without mentioning what was said by one or another individually, as there are particular reasons for this.

There is still a full memory of the son alive today, and a memory of the father which has not yet faded completely. And we were glad to meet with this memory as with a living force for the present day. . . .

The old father, Johann Christoph Blumhardt, came from the mission school in Basel and from old pietist circles, into a parish dominated by much unbelief and superstition. He had a great love for the people and was extremely faithful in visiting them in their houses; in this way he concerned himself with all of them. Yet because of his background he kept a comprehensive view of the whole world.

When it came to a tremendous conflict with unbelief and all these things,[1] his view broadened afresh. He saw clearly that if Jesus was to win victories here, this victory was not only to have significance for Möttlingen and the little congregation there, a victory in which Jesus conquered a possessed woman; but in this victory the Devil was to be thrown back all along the line, into the utmost parts of the world; this victory was to have the greatest significance for all of world history. The struggle was a struggle for the Kingdom of God, a struggle for the light to conquer the darkness, for Jesus to become Victor. This little victory was to have its effect on the whole world. Here something had to happen which would bring a basic defeat to the whole demonic world, so that the Devil's works would not come up again, and this not only in Möttlingen, but throughout the world.

In the pietism of Württemberg a strong and deep direction had developed which stood very much in contrast to the superficial evangelical movement. Through Bengel and Öttinger, as well as through Beck, a deep interpretation of the eschatological powers was given, so that one cannot speak of any subjectivism in those circles with which Johann Christoph Blumhardt had contact. When Öttinger said, "The ultimate of all things is corporeality"; when again and

[1] These words of Eberhard, taken down in shorthand in German and transcribed, were probably never corrected by him.

again Beck's words speak so decisively of the greatness of God's Kingdom; it becomes clear that in those days pietism was not nearly so subjective as the pietism of today.

It was clear to Blumhardt that he had to take an even broader view than that of Öttinger, Bengel and Beck. People were healed; devils were driven out; emotional illnesses were cured. It finally went so far that Möttlingen had to be left behind.

Friends helped in the purchase of a royal spa, the property of King William and Queen Pauline of Württemberg. Even today the letters W and P stand above the entrance; Blumhardt interpreted them to stand for "Wait and Press on."[2]

Now he came to Bad Boll. Besides his wife and children, he also took along Gottliebin [Dittus] and her brother and also [Theodor] Brodersen, who later married Gottliebin. Little by little a small community of fifty people, including children, was formed, living and working together. . . . In the course of time father Blumhardt became more and more free of the healing of the sick, and during the last years of his life he did not heal many people.

The friends told us that the father, and also the son, very carefully guarded the laying on of hands; it was free from any kind of magical power or sorcery and never could become mixed with it in any way. Both Blumhardts, the father and the son, refused to have anything to do with this power. Just as baptism in itself achieves nothing at all unless the new birth has already taken place, as we saw today, so it is also with the healing of sicknesses. Not even the tiniest bit of physical-emotional influence or current can be tolerated here. Rather, it is an expression of faith.

And of what faith? It is the faith that in the healing,

[2] *Warte und Pressiere.*

however hard it is, in the driving out of devils, however fiendish they are, the immediate personal relationship makes no difference. Here the Church is needed. The laying on of hands is the sign that God is using the Church for a decisive act of faith in which *God* does something tremendous.

Through this the father, Johann Christoph, already in his day came to the forgiveness of sins through the authority of the Church with the laying on of hands, the forgiveness which he pronounced in the Name of Jesus Christ. It is significant that the healing of the sick diminished more and more during the last years of his life; for there was a danger that the character of a prayer-healing institution would come into the foreground. The son continued the healings for a time, but not for very long.

There were several sons of Johann Christoph Blumhardt. Two were especially outstanding, Theophil and Christoph. Theophil was the one of whom it was assumed that he would be the successor to his father. At first no one thought anything special of Christoph. When he returned home from the University of Tübingen and asked what he should do, his father said, "Well, you've been living in such a grand style, I can't use you. You can wash bottles." And he put him in the wine cellar. "You can't live with us; you can be a guest."

So he washed bottles, etc., for about half a year; the father then felt that Christoph might yet amount to something. He gradually drew him into things. Toward the end of the father's life all were very anxious to know to whom the real service would be given. The father said, "It is Christoph." Theophil became a pastor in a village near Bad Boll, and the actual service was given to Christoph.

At first he worked completely in the manner of his father. He came to breakfast in his dressing gown and then spoke with the people in the old, pietistic way.... Gradually a new vision of God's Kingdom grew in him. I asked all kinds of people what was the essential difference between the father and the son Blumhardt. What finally came out of it was that basically there was no essential difference. True, the father disclosed the power of evil and stood in the midst of a sharp personal fight against evil; whereas the son, while maintaining this fighting position, nevertheless wanted to see how God accomplishes His victories *in the world*. There is a distinction here; but let us not forget that the father regarded this fight [with evil] as a historical event over the whole earth. He believed that real victories of the Spirit had been won even before the Last Judgment.

Blumhardt the son freed himself more and more from the pious language, from the organized Church, and from pietism. He said he had had to give up these three things. The result of this freeing was that he now had an ear to discern in the history of the world where God wanted to show the Kingdom of Justice, the victory over evil spirits. He had the impression that "nothing can be expected of the pious people." He expected it from the "farmer lads," not from the pious.... And so he looked around more and more to see whether the victory of Jesus wouldn't make itself felt among the non-pious.

He was not a Social Democrat in the ordinary sense.... He was, however, a loyal Social Democrat in the sense that he felt here a foreshadowing of the Kingdom of Justice....

He saw the help for the working people in the manifestation of God's Kingdom. In *this* way he wanted a victory over the demonic powers to be won; this was what concerned him. The result was that the pietists turned away from him....

I do not believe that he would be very pleased about the fact that his books are read in such large numbers and that so many people cite Bad Boll; for he was extremely sad whenever he was imitated. That is why he warned everybody again and again neither to imitate nor to overestimate Bad Boll as a place, and not to overestimate Christoph Blumhardt. His warning was of no use; and still he never found a *true* recognition. . . .

Christoph Blumhardt himself had several sons. . . . One of them became a doctor; he was an uncommonly altruistic person. In him the proclamation of his grandfather and father was still at work in such a way that he had a very loving approach to people. . . . None of Christoph Blumhardt's sons became his successor, and thus it came about that the Moravians took it upon themselves to administer Bad Boll in the spirit of Blumhardt, and the present housefather is endeavoring to do this in a sincere way.

We heard several testimonies from people who had lived with Blumhardt. One concerns the communal work. There were sulfur pits, and two workers had unfortunately left the blow lamp down there. When they went down again to fetch it, gases had developed and the mechanic called up for some brandy to be given to them. And now Blumhardt fetched the gardener and the gardener climbed down and brought one of the men up. When he went down a second time to fetch the other man, he himself succumbed to the poisoning, while the other man died of the effects of hydrogen sulfide.

Now Blumhardt, for the rest of his life, cared for Mrs. Ehrath, the wife of the gardener. It took her four and a half years to recover from this blow. Blumhardt bought her a boarding house in Freudenstadt, through which she was to be provided for the rest of her life. This woman received very strong impressions from the life and witness in Bad Boll and she told me a great deal. She was particularly glad about my witness; she said it was a witness like that in the time of Blumhardt. This was a story by a member of the household.

There was also the son of a university professor, who had taught the theory of relativity already before Einstein. This man had suffered heavy depressions in his youth. He had gotten to know the demonic powers in a frightful way already in his youth, so that he had been in serious danger of taking his own life. From his parental home he had been endowed with the best faith, but he was a pessimist by disposition. His depressions alternated with periods of exuberance during which he felt like a demi-god. The intervals between the periods of depression and exuberance he spent in melancholy, and in these periods he produced his scientific works. However, these intervals were quite short.

This man came to Bad Boll after having lived in this unbearable condition for many years. In Bad Boll he encountered Jesus, and the Spirit of Power freed him from his demonism. He was redeemed and liberated, a man aglow with fire. I saw this man myself, and he read his story to me, from ten closely written pages. To be quite exact, he confided in me as in a father confessor. He felt such a strong affinity that he sought me out again and again to talk things over with me. This was an absolutely unforgettable hour for me. Of course this old doctor of philosophy is not healed in the sense that the sickness is no longer noticeable at all. But he is able to work and no longer needs sedatives....

These are miraculous things, and there are many to be

seen. This man said to me, among other things, "If Christoph Blumhardt were alive today, he would undoubtedly no longer be a member of the Social Democratic Party. For it no longer represents justice for the working class as it did at that time."

The closer circle of Blumhardt friends, which consists of only a few hundred people, does not belong to the Religious-Social League or to the religious socialists, and they feel certain misgivings about this group, for two reasons. The religious socialists took from Christoph Blumhardt's witness its relevance to the social message, and they made this the main thing. Whereas Christoph Blumhardt expected everything from the Holy Spirit, also for Social Democracy; the Social Democrats, on the other hand, are in danger of expecting everything from their politics. Blumhardt did not think this way at all; he expected, for the Social Democrats as well as for everybody else, an act of creation, a powerful intervention in history.

In regard to the Church and unity, Christoph Blumhardt had freed himself more and more from the organized Church. However, he did not experience a real unity of the Church-community in his circle, except in rare instances. Much was still lacking here. The fact that the essential nature of God's Kingdom must be manifested through the Church-community was glimpsed, but this was not attained. ... The Blumhardts knew, however, that their authority to approach all events and occurrences in the Name of Jesus Christ came from the Church of God.

The great thing, as Leonhard Ragaz showed above all, is that here was a man who did not live in the completeness of his own power; it was a fire from Jesus, a likeness of Jesus, that radiated from him. Here was a man who saw and expected something from God for all life's problems and for every historical event; a man who had the great vision for the whole of God's Kingdom and who yet took pains for, and stood up for, every individual.

Blumhardt the father and Blumhardt the son were both men who lived completely for the Kingdom of God; for them the objective reality and the greatness of God's Kingdom was more important than anything else. At the same time they had a deep personal love for each individual person. They always saw the objective reality of the cause, yet they did not despise the subjective personal faith.

Later, the sick were healed without the laying on of hands. "If people expect a magic effect from the laying on of hands, then let them be healed when I only preach." The faith of healing remained.

The children loved Blumhardt very much. He gathered them around him daily and blessed them, laying his hands on them. The children could not misunderstand this.

Soon after this visit to Bad Boll came spring, and the work of building had to be pushed, since more and more people had announced their intention of coming.

The year 1932 was a real year of building up. Guests came, especially young people. On the day of our Tata's death Annemarie came to stay, after having come on a visit in the summer of 1931. Students from Tübingen visited us, stimulated by Hardi, who was studying there, and by Karl Heim's positive interest in our way. Edith, too, was there in the holidays. The Mathis family left Switzerland to come to us, and other Swiss visitors came. Hans and Margrit Meier came as a young married couple, also Gerhard Wiegand and others stayed on. Our dear Ria came, who had read about us and seen pictures in the *Deutsche Sonntagspost* (German Sunday Newspaper);

August Dyroff also came, and Josef Stängl decided to stay.

There were people from very different backgrounds. Our Marie Eckardt,[3] an older deaconess, came from moved Christian evangelical groups. Another older sister who came to us was our Mother Elsbeth,[4] whose daughter Hildegard had already come some years earlier and is still with us. There were Catholics and Protestants; there were some who had been homeless for years; there were those of left-wing and right-wing political opinions. The questions which the different people brought with them were fought out among us in sometimes warm discussions under the great beech tree where we used to gather after the day's burden and work. Many times something broke through among us and gave an answer, coming from Christ and the Church, which placed everything in a far higher light.

[3] Marie died at our Evergreen Community (near Norfolk, Conn.) in January 1963.

[4] Elsbeth Friedrich died in Primavera, Paraguay, in July 1961.

## CONFLICT WITH HITLER'S STATE

THE NAZI SPIRIT was already very much alive in many people in Germany. "It can't go on like this! We need a dictator! Hitler must come to power! National interest is higher than self-interest!" All this sounded fine, but those who saw deeper realized, through other words of Hitler's, the great danger which he brought to the German people. And yet—was Bolshevism any better? That summer of 1932 we still had hope that these two dangers, National Socialism and Bolshevism, would pass.

It was through a call from Heini, who was studying at an agricultural school in Fulda, that we first heard, on January 30, 1933, that Hitler had been appointed Chancellor of the German Reich and that he had already taken office. This was a great shock for us, for we had a presentiment of what might lie ahead of us.

When the decrees and changes came out each day, we knew more and more that we could not expect anything good. *Gleichschaltung* ("equalization," or enforced conformity to everything in National Socialism) of all in the state and persecution of the Jews were among the first things we heard about. Schools, monasteries, communities were closed down because they did not want to be "equalized." All Germans were told they had to give the greeting, "Heil Hitler." Most people in different walks of life complied with this, thinking there was no other way. It was a pitiful sight when, for example, an old lady like our own Grandmother Arnold gave this greeting, or when a university professor or teacher greeted his students in lecture hall or classroom with the words, "Heil Hitler." Anyone who did not do this was despised as a "traitor to the people and enemy of the Fatherland."

Already in those early days we heard of Jews running the gauntlet. Everything was supposed to be the fault of the Jews. At the entrances to villages, placards were put up saying "No admittance for dogs and Jews." Germans were no longer allowed to buy from Jews. In some places, as for example in Kassel, a barbed wire fence was set up, and everyone who bought from a Jew was denounced and locked inside it. The race question played an important part. The Nordic, Germanic race! Everyone had to prove his Aryan descent, and marriage between one of Jewish or part-Jewish descent and an Aryan was no longer allowed. Some mixed marriages already existing were annulled. This caused a great deal of suffering. Those Jews who were able to emigrate to other countries tried to do so. But it was far from simple—often impossible—to obtain the necessary papers.

There were a number, including Eberhard, who saw through the spirit of the Hitler movement in the beginning, and even in advance. The SS, SA, and Hitler Youth marched through villages and towns with their songs, especially *Die Fahne hoch.*[1] One could hear this Nazi song being sung everywhere and with enthusiasm. Such aggressive groups came marching through our Rhön Bruderhof too, for it was soon realized that we were not willing to cooperate. In many a brotherhood meeting the

[1] "Raise high the flag," known as the *Horst Wessel* song.

question was to what extent we should give an opposite witness. We wished to act openly at all times. We could not say "Heil Hitler," nor would we be "equalized," that is, accept all decrees, etc. Very often Eberhard went to the authorities to explain our position—that the discipleship of Christ as we understood it could not go together with the demands of National Socialism. Also that we could not say "Heil Hitler," since we did not believe that the *Heil* (salvation) came from Hitler! This often got us into trouble on the street or at business.

Already in those first months we heard about the closing of schools, particularly modern ones; about people being removed to concentration camps; about opposition to the churches, Catholic as well as Protestant. Free speech was forbidden. Everything came under censorship. These conditions were just right for the flourishing of hypocrisy! No publicity was given to all the things that were actually happening. There would just be short notices, such as, "Another Communist nest discovered!"

The question before us, then, was what we should do. In the brotherhood we agreed to try to continue building up, to live the witness entrusted to us nevertheless, and to speak out where necessary. "It will depend on who holds out the longest," said Eberhard.

So we continued to build. During the spring and summer of 1933 we had many guests and helpers, including some who wanted to join us for good and go the way of discipleship to the end. One of these was our Günther Homann,[2] who worked faithfully with us for many years in our library and archives. At Easter, then, we held the baptism of a group of these people who had recently come to us and who wanted to go the way of the Cross together with us. Among them were Hans and

[2] Günther Homann died in Primavera, Paraguay, on September 6, 1957.

Margrit Meier, Peter and Anni Mathis, Edith Boecker (later
Arnold),[3] Susi (now Fros), Gertrud (now Arnold), our Hans
Hermann and our Monika. There were eighteen altogether
who took this serious step with us at this critical time. This
gave the whole group new courage and strengthened us on the
road we had taken.

The discussions with guests were very lively, and often one
felt that every word mattered. It was no wonder that a number
who had asked for the novitiate left us when things seemed to
be getting more difficult or dangerous—our "summer novices"!

Our life went on. We held the wedding of Kurt and
Marianne. This wedding was carried out in spite of many a
struggle with the relatives, especially Marianne's. A trip which
I took to visit Marianne's mother turned out quite negative.
Marianne's relatives had even accepted help from the Nazis.
Still, all this did not prevent us from going ahead, and the
wedding took place.

Our Edith was pressed by her parents to come home to
Hamburg at least once, to say goodbye. Since she did not agree
with her parents, she was locked up and her money for the
trip back to the Bruderhof was taken away from her. So in
the night she let herself down by a rope from the second story
of a town house in Hamburg, to travel by roundabout ways to
the community. Similar things happened with others, who also
went through a real break with their families. But now it had
to be all or nothing.

Just about this time, Eberhard was confined to bed for
several weeks, after an operation in Fulda. He had suffered
a broken leg, a bad and complicated fracture.

It was in these same days that Hitler called a plebiscite to
get the people to express support for his politics and actions.

[3] Edith died in Primavera in April 1943.

This was probably done because other nations refused to believe that the whole German people would stand behind this government, for in other countries they heard more news about the terror, the concentration camps and all the rest, than we in Germany heard. It was not a free election; it was closely watched. Everyone was compelled to go to the polls, and they made a point of informing us of this. We agreed that we could not simply say "No" like anarchists; we felt we had to give an answer which would give a positive witness to our attitude.

Eberhard then formulated a sentence which said that we would support a government that was appointed by God, but that our mission was a different one; our task was to live according to the way and example of Christ, as a corrective for this world. Each one copied this sentence onto a piece of gummed paper. Then we all went together down to Veitstein-bach, the village in whose district we belonged. Each of us pasted this piece of paper on the ballot and threw it into the urn. To our astonishment the newspaper announced afterwards that everybody had answered "Yes" in this plebiscite, in affirmation of Hitler's politics!

Four days later, on November 16, our Hof was surrounded by about 140 men, SS, SA and Gestapo. No one was allowed to leave his room or place of work, and at every door stood one of these men. Then they pushed their way into the rooms and searched everything. Books, letters, even personal letters of engaged and married couples were read and sometimes made fun of. Particular attention was paid to letters from other countries, such as those from Hardi, who had gone to England (at the invitation of John Stephens, a Quaker friend), since for reasons of conscience he could not sign the papers that were necessary to continue his studies in Tübingen. This was a very difficult situation; those outside of Germany knew more about conditions in Germany than we who lived there. Information of this kind from the outside was called "horror propaganda" against Germany, and this was subject to severe punishment as treason.

To continue: They searched longest, of course, in Eberhard's study, in the archives and library, looking for writings and records "hostile to the State." Eberhard himself lay on the sofa with his newly-operated leg while these people pushed their way in and searched. They probably would have liked to take Eberhard away at that time and put him in a concentration camp. But what could they do with this sick man? Late that evening a big car drove off loaded with books, writings and records. What would happen next?

It was then that Eberhard wrote the song, "The dark cohorts of raging power," which we sang often in those days, to the tune of "A mighty fortress is our God." As dedication Eberhard wrote, "A song of the fighting Church; to its housemother, his Emmy, and to all her children of the Church-community, after November 16, 1933."

> The dark cohorts of raging power
> Now grasp for steel and armor.
> Its avalanche would overwhelm
> And swallow Christian witness.
> The State of towering might,
> It claims now every right
> Completely and entire,
> Grips Altar, Throne, and all.
> Who will withstand it finally?
>
> The Light of God is Jesus Christ;
> It blazes forth as witness.
> Its banner bright is fervent love,

And unity its daily gift.
In living and in death
Encircled, linked and bound,
God's Church as one is held,
And clasps the enemy
To encompass him by love alone.

The fight breaks out as flaming brand
That scatters sparks and embers;
From land to land its beacon flares,
A bright and never-setting star.
For all men through great strife
Christ's suffering comes to life;
The Living God restores;
His judgment now appears,
The greatest hour for all the earth.

God's heart is only glowing light,
Love is His greatest power.
The Church drawn heavenward by His love
Is freed to seek the Spirit.
And neither force nor law,
No pressure and no death,
Nor snatching from our midst
Of our pure little ones
Can drive away Christ's Spirit.

Rejecting hate, the brotherhood
Now can respect the enemy
And freely face him eye to eye
To serve alone the side of love.
No power of the polls,
No ensign of the State,
No might of arms and war

Nor monstrous glittering face,
Shall harm the vision of our Christ.

Now striding forth the band sets out
In unity, in strength and peace.
Unhindered by all earthly goods,
She praises God in joyful song.
Her covenant renewed,
The hour—God's history.
Seed of His future reign
Now flower from out His pain
And honor Him eternally.

From this moment on we were watched more closely. First
the school superintendent of the district of Fulda, who had
formerly been very kindly disposed toward us, came to give
our children a test to find out if they had been "patriotically"
instructed. They were also expected to sing for him the Hitler
songs, including the well-known Horst Wessel Song. Of course
they did not know it, and so they did not pass the test. The
consequence was that our school was closed down and after
Christmas we were to get Nazi teachers. Furthermore, the
children and young people whose parents did not live with
us were to be taken away.

Thus we had to act fast to get them out of Germany. We
tried Switzerland first. Passports would have to be obtained
and their guardians would have to give permission, or rather
they would have to help by obtaining the documents themselves,
for we would certainly not be able to get these papers in Fulda.
The District Administrator, von Gagern, who had been so
friendly to us, had been replaced, and the new one, a former
veterinarian, was a stern Nazi; in fact it was he who issued
the orders against us.

Unfortunately, we did not succeed in getting this help from guardians or relatives for all the children; some of them were fearful of getting into trouble by doing this. So some of the children had to leave us, which was really quite painful for us. Among these were Edgar Zimmermann, Heinz Schultheiss, the four Helwig children, and others. Our little gypsy boy Erhardt too was fetched away by his father, as I told earlier. It was the same way with Moni's little Ulala, who came from "traveling folk." That was a short, sad farewell! We heard later that he died in a Catholic home for boys.

We were so much the happier, then, for each child that could stay with us. These children left for Switzerland with Lene Schulz and Annemarie early in January 1934. When the Nazi teacher turned up after the Christmas holidays, there were no school children there for him to teach!

Of course, all this caused us many difficulties. It was all but impossible to send young people out for education. They all had to break off their training, or could not begin it, as everything was "equalized." This meant that they all were required to join the groups established by the Nazis—the Hitler Youth, and so on. Most young people in Germany did this with great enthusiasm, since a lot was done for them: "To youth belongs the future!"

Many other difficulties were also put in our way. Restrictions were placed on our contact with visitors. No one was allowed to stay overnight with us. We could only have "members" who were willing to commit themselves to stay for at least half a year. This was often difficult, since it was hard to know beforehand which ones ought to commit themselves.

Besides these things, our financial situation was also made much more difficult. In the first place, we were told that the mortgage on our house of 15,000 marks, which had been loaned us for twenty years, had to be paid back within fourteen days! Where were we to get the money from? We were no longer allowed to sell our turnery or the books and other writings published by us. The state support we had been receiving for the school and the poor was stopped immediately. (Until that time many tramps had come to us.) Thus we really had no income anymore. We were able to sell almost none of our farm products, since we needed them so badly for our large household of 180 people. But in those years we did have a great joy in the babies that were given to our newly founded families. This was an especial encouragement. Eberhard and I also got our first grandchildren, Heidi and Hans Benedikt.

Early in 1934 we had really taken a chance in sending our school children to Switzerland. Now we were threatened with losing our young people as well, and so it was time to look for a place outside of Germany for them. To begin with, two brothers were sent to Switzerland, but they did not succeed, for it was felt there that they had enough people of this kind already.

Marie Schmidt's home for children in Switzerland, which had sheltered our children for a short period, now asked us to take them away again. So Eberhard and I were then sent to look for a place for them, Eberhard with a walking cast on his leg, which had not been helped at all by the many journeys of that year! Eberhard had had a vision that the little land of Liechtenstein should be our next step, and so we went to this little principality between Switzerland, Austria and Germany. We stayed in a little village inn in Schaan, in the valley, with the idea of first getting to know the people of Liechtenstein and learning to follow their way of speaking. We did not mention politics or our difficulties under the Nazis, but we did tell them that we wanted to have a home for children there.

While we were engrossed in conversation, someone mentioned the summer hotel at Silum, 1,500 meters (5,000 feet) high, which since the previous summer had not been used much. Eberhard and I then went to see the owner, and he was willing to lease it to us.

The hotel had not been used all winter, and the roads and paths were totally covered by snow. It was already the beginning of March (1934), and we were advised to wait with our trip there at least until some of the snow was melted. However, we had no time to wait, since the director of the children's home in Switzerland needed the room urgently for other children who had applied previously, and our children had to move out. A friendly farmer from Triesenberg told us he would give us a ride up there in his sleigh. We had also asked Adolf Braun, who just happened to be on a trip in Switzerland selling books, to go up with us.

It was a dangerous trip, as our driver himself said, for it was very steep, and we had to go through deep snow without being able to see where the road was. On the way he told us that many vehicles had already come to grief there! However, he thought he would be able to find the way. And so we traveled up this adventurous road, not quite without anxiety, yet aware that it was necessary to find a place for our children. It went quite well, but the driver could not take us all the way to the hotel; so Eberhard had to make his way through deep snow and deep holes as best he could, with his plaster cast.

When we arrived up there, we found the owner of the hotel and went through the hotel with him, looking out for the possibilities of the house as we went. Everything was not perfect, especially in regard to the heating. Yet on the whole it was a splendid place, surrounded by the high, snow-covered Alps. Nearby, a few minutes' walk higher up, there was also a little house, a Swiss cottage, as it was called, which we could perhaps rent, and also several mountain huts. Altogether room could be made for a hundred people.

The trip back on the steep road was especially dangerous because the tracks of our sleigh had been almost obliterated by the wind. Before we set out, however, we shook hands with the owner of the hotel on the agreement that we were to move into the beautiful hotel at Silum as soon as possible. He informed us of the annual rent and asked for advance payment of half of the amount. For us, who had nothing, this meant quite a large sum—it was about 1,500 francs—and we would have to get the money quickly. (The following night I had a bad dream, that we all had tumbled down the mountain.) The children had to leave the children's home, and then there was the whole move of this little group of about ten to twelve children and grown-ups. Many things had to be taken up there as well, especially food.

The next morning, then, Eberhard and I traveled to Chur, where we wanted to visit friends. Eberhard did not go everywhere with me, since he would have had to take a car on account of his weak leg and we had no money. So sometimes we went separately. I decided to go alone, then, to visit Julia Lerchy in the hospital. The previous summer she had been at the Rhön Bruderhof and, with a number of other guests, had been there when we celebrated Eberhard's fiftieth birthday.

Because of back trouble our Julia had to lie flat on her back, yet she was very lively and interested. She was quite shocked to hear what we had to report to her about all that had happened to us since she left us in August 1933. I told her all about our situation. She reminded me of how we had still gone on courageously building in the summer and had enlarged the dining room, and because of this had celebrated Hardi's engagement to Edith Boecker in the attic. It had impressed her very much that in spite of all the difficulties we encountered we wanted to go on building as if we were to go on living there all the time, but also to be ready at any time to leave it all. We also thought of a similar saying of Luther's: "If I knew that the world would be destroyed tomorrow, I would still plant my apple tree today." This was the direction of our thoughts then, and also of our talks.

When I took leave of Julia, she asked me to come again in the afternoon with Eberhard. The two of us together had a very good talk with the sick woman, during which she told us that she wished to come and join the Bruderhof. When we said goodbye she pressed an envelope into our hands. On opening it outside, we found 8,000 francs, to our great joy and gratitude to God—given to us in this particular moment by someone from whom we had not expected it at all. Now we could pay the first installment; we could pay for the move, and the fuel and food for the group, and furthermore could send the larger part of the sum to the hard-pressed Rhön Bruderhof! How ashamed I was of my little faith, which was expressed in the dream I had had!

The move took place with Adolf's help, while Eberhard and I visited other friends, friends belonging to the religious-social movement. For the first time we also visited Essertines, where we met Madame Rossier, the wife of the founder. We felt a true spirit of community in her, and we were glad we could get to know her.

There were two points on which our opinions differed. They believed in celibacy, feeling that in such a serious time we should live for the Kingdom alone. Marriage was felt to be a diversion. Even couples who were already married did not live together. Another important point on which we differed was the military question, for they believed in defensive war.

What impressed us most was their attitude to communal work. While discussions of an inner nature were going on, quiet work was done, such as weaving market baskets, braiding onions in long strings, and so on. We did not feel anything disturbing in this, for we noticed with what concentration they still took part in the discussions. At the end of our visit, Madame Rossier gave us material help in money and food for the beginning at our new Bruderhof. A second visit which Monika and I made there about half a year later did not turn out so well, as there was more emphasis on the differences.

We also went to Mother Mathis, called Nona,[4] who had taken very loving care of our Hans Hermann during the winter months, when he was ill with tuberculosis. Now we could take our boy, who was very much better, with us to the Alm Bruderhof, as we now called the new Bruderhof.

Wonderful days followed of reunion with our children and with some of the other young people, who arrived there little by little. What a welcoming that was! Escaped from the snares of the Nazis!

Families were also sent over to help, for instance Kleiners and Zimmermanns, as well as some young people. Hardi came from England, to continue his studies in Zurich. With him came a group of English people who wanted to venture into the new life with us on the basis of the witness of the Sermon on the Mount. Arnold and Gladys Mason came as a young married couple, and Kathleen Hamilton (now Hasenberg),

[4] Margarita Mathis, mother of Peter Mathis, joined the community later. She died in Primavera, Paraguay, on June 21, 1954.

and Winifred Bridgwater (now Dyroff) with her parents, who came with the intention of getting to know the group which their daughter wanted to join.

This was a very moving time—it was the first time people had come to us from England—and we had very deep-going talks with them. Especially memorable for me was the way these people gave in their belongings, in particular two rings with precious stones (diamonds), which I believe were the young couple's engagement rings. We had moving times with this group, although most of us had more or less forgotten our school English. Hardi acted as interpreter and did this very well.

The wedding of Hardi and Edith also took place about that time. They had gotten to know one another as students at Tübingen. This wedding was a special experience for us. "Christ the Head" was the theme that was given to Eberhard for this wedding.

Eberhard and I were not able to stay much longer at the Alm Bruderhof after this. We felt very strongly that we belonged in that place where the need and the danger was greatest. So we stayed at our old Bruderhof (Rhön) for the winter of 1934–1935. There we were also able to celebrate our silver wedding anniversary on December 20, with great joy, together with the brotherhood. Eberhard had put together a little book and signed it "The Bridegroom." A garland of silver thistles hung in the middle of the dining room, adorned with twenty-five tall white candles. Much love was shown to us from all sides. It was to be the last wedding anniversary we could celebrate together!

At about this time there came a telephone call from Heini at the Alm Bruderhof, with the question whether he might become engaged to Annemarie Wächter. (This was not quite unexpected for us.) So they were able to celebrate their engagement, too, in those days. On our wedding anniversary, as well as on my fiftieth birthday, Eberhard read out passages from our letters at the time of our engagement. All these things are very much alive in my memory. Also that on our wedding anniversary in 1933 our first grandson, Hans Benedikt, was born. In the midst of a time that was so heavy and dark for the many people who had to suffer, we were still allowed such a fullness of experience!

Very soon after Christmas the question of military service came up. Germany was to be mobilized again, as we were informed in all the daily papers. Hans Meier, who was in Switzerland just then, called us up to tell us that the law was now to go into effect and that the first age groups would have to register.

That same night we had a long meeting of the brotherhood in which we tried to become clear about what we should do. Had the hour come for us to suffer for the resistance? Or did we feel our task was to continue building up, on the Alm Bruderhof for instance, where men were very much needed for the work? If I remember rightly, there were seventeen at that time who would have to register for military service sooner or later, some of them novices. After a time of silence to ask God for the right guidance in this hour, we decided to send the young men in question to the Alm Bruderhof that same night—by rail, bicycle, or on foot, by different routes, since we did not have the means to send them all by railroad.

The next morning everything was very quiet on the Hof! No more school children! Practically no young brothers (at least none of German nationality)! Soon we heard that all of them had arrived safely, one by one, and that each time another one arrived there was great rejoicing.

Hermann Arnold, a nephew of Eberhard's, who came to us somewhat later, became convinced that he had to leave the SA (Hitler's storm troops) for reasons of conscience. He then joined this group of young men at the Alm Bruderhof. (Hermann's mother, our Tante Käthe, also came to us later and taught in our school for sixteen years, until her death in Paraguay in 1956.)

Now we had to watch for better possibilities for these young men and their families—those of them who were married. For at the Alm Bruderhof it was not possible to expand much. Also, we did not know how much longer we with our peace witness would be tolerated in Germany.

So we decided on journeys in Switzerland. Eberhard was also asked by the brotherhood to travel to Holland and England, mainly to look for new possibilities for a better place for the community, but also to raise funds for a better means of earning a living for the Alm Bruderhof and its members. Hardi was asked to accompany Eberhard on this trip, because Eberhard's leg was not yet healed, and also because of the contacts Hardi had made in England during the year he was studying there.

Both Eberhard and Hardi were much impressed by how moved people were in Holland, as they found out in this time which they experienced together. From their letters and from a report in which Hardi summarized this trip, it was clearly evident that the whole journey was very difficult for Eberhard. This was partly on account of his leg, since they had little money and he often had to walk considerable distances; but also on account of the lack of understanding by many people for the hard struggle the brotherhood was having, especially at the Rhön Bruderhof where there was daily danger.

Since a number of the young fathers had left on that night

for the Alm Bruderhof because of the military service question, we now decided to hire a cheap bus, so that their families could join them there. There were several little babies with their mothers. Elisabeth Zumpe, Renata Zimmermann, Michel Gneiting and Hans Martin were laid two by two in little baskets. There were also some toddlers and three- and four-year-olds, some older persons, and still others to help. I also went along, as housemother.

Very early in the morning the group set out in this very bumpy bus with hardly any springs. Many of the children had a bad time, and so we had to stop often. It was quite an undertaking, after all. When we arrived at the border some time before midnight, we were at first refused entry. There were a number of telephone calls back and forth, and finally we were allowed through. Another victory! Emi-Ma, whose little Elisabeth was only 17 days old, was not well at all, and so we had to stop for another night somewhere in Switzerland. We found a place where I could stay with Emi-Ma and Elisabeth. The place was very simple and without any heating whatsoever, and it was a cold night late in March. We put the baby to bed in our suitcase and soon went to bed ourselves too. Next morning a very obliging lady helped us to start on our way again. Meantime the group with all the little children drove on through the night and reached their goal early in the morning; there they were lovingly received and cared for. We traveled on during the day and arrived later. What an undertaking that journey was!

Eberhard, returning from England, also went to the Alm Bruderhof first, since the help he had received was mainly for the building up of the Alm Bruderhof, especially help from the Quakers for a greenhouse. Because of the short summer in the high altitude there (1,500 meters, or nearly 5,000 feet), a greenhouse was absolutely necessary for raising vegetables.

There were many discussions now as to how the rest of the money, somewhat more than nine hundred pounds, could best be put to use for the community. We decided to lease some land 1,000 meters lower, down in the Rhine valley.

On this valley land we raised fine vegetables! The trip up and down, often daily, was very strenuous for the brothers. I remember how Fritz Kleiner used to climb directly down the steep mountainside to avoid the roundabout way with its many turns. Once another brother called after him, "Surely you don't want to go down by that steep, rocky mountainside?" To which Fritz answered, "Well, we don't want to go the way the whole world goes!" And he went on his way.

The wedding of Christian and our Sophie was a special experience at this time and brought us all very close together. Hardi and Edith, who were both studying and copying old manuscripts in Zurich, came up for this occasion. It was the last wedding Eberhard conducted.

Very soon Eberhard left for the Rhön Bruderhof, this time alone. He wanted to be there for Whitsunday; also there were some, especially those from Bernhard Jansa's group at Eisenach, who had been with us for nearly a year and wanted to be united with us through baptism. Eberhard then came back again soon, for this newly established community had its difficulties.

There was many a struggle which came about through modern Hutterianism with its services and offices and the fact that some were not always in agreement with this. There was often a tension. On the one hand there was the Church developing freely through the Spirit; on the other hand, the orders and traditions of the present-day Hutterians. It got to the point where some wanted to read and hear nothing but Hutterian teachings and writings. Others wanted to read and hear only what the Spirit was saying and speaking to men today.

Some, like myself, were between these two extremes. I felt an understanding for Hutterianism and what it had grown to be; yet I did not want by any means to do without that which had broken in among us in such a living way through all the years. In a talk at the Rhön Bruderhof, Eberhard once said, "If we are going to read nothing but the old teachings of the Hutterians [precious to him] and force people to accept them, then I will not take part in this!" We had quite a struggle against a real rigidity in our circle.

Just at this time our first grandson in Hardi's family was born, Eberhard Klaus. On the third day his mother, Edith, fell ill with a serious vein infection and childbed fever. Her life was threatened, and at times it looked as if it would be extinguished. She lived in one of our mountain huts, and the nursing was quite difficult. The baby was well; he looked around in the world with his innocent eyes, not knowing what was happening around him.

This serious illness went together with the inner struggle of the community and was fought through at the same time. We saw that in both cases life was being threatened by the powers of death which struck at the innermost being of every single one of us. This went on for several weeks. The life power which triumphed in Edith was also victorious over the deathly power of law which threatened us and into which we were in danger of sliding. That freedom which is given to us over and over again in Romans 8 triumphed here too! Yes, in all the years following, this same fight has been with us ever again.

# EBERHARD'S LAST STRUGGLE

SHORTLY AFTER Eberhard's last birthday, which we celebrated at the Alm Bruderhof, we felt very much urged to return to our home Bruderhof. The young people gave the wonderful Tolstoi play they had been practicing, "Where Love Is, God Is." In the brotherhood it was decided that finally a specialist should see to Eberhard's leg, since in spite of the cast it seemed to us to be quite crooked, and walking was very difficult and painful for him.

In those last days before our departure from the Alm Bruderhof, Eberhard was very fond of looking at the world of the stars through a good telescope which a member had brought with him. Often we were both engrossed in observing the larger world, instead of our little planet, as the center of God's great creation. He showed me Saturn, the planet surrounded by rings of light. I remembered talks with Eberhard on the subject: Where are our loved ones who have died? And I wondered if Eberhard was thinking that perhaps soon he would be on one of these stars.

We were often concerned with thoughts about the great star world, also with the Revelation to John, which he read out and spoke about in those days, also some visions of the prophets, such as Daniel and Ezekiel. We felt that the connection between the course of the historical hour in which we were living and the future, the final end of world history, had moved very close; we also felt it as a grace that we were placed into this time. In a number of *Gemeindestunden* (inner meetings) we were pointed to God's great future. It was a great pain for Eberhard that we were often too small, too mean and miserable, to see all these happenings in a greater light with the eyes of God.

After our return to the Rhön Bruderhof it was this that pained him very much. Nothing very bad had actually happened. What pained him in particular was certain emotional, all-too-human relationships between members at the Rhön Bruderhof. There was very little listening or feeling for God's speaking in our time. Eberhard tried to impress this on us through the history of the martyrs of the sixteenth century; through the Rosicrucians (since there was then a serious representative of these among us); through the whole world situation, including the special situation of Germany in this time of tyranny. But at that moment people did not have a listening ear; they were not receptive to what this time had to say to us. They loved human goodness, and so sometimes they coddled one another instead of correcting one another.

So it naturally came about that there was also talking about others behind their backs. All values were much too emotional, too human. And this at a time when we were seriously threatened from without because of our spiritual witness! It reminded one of the hour when Jesus again and again found his three most beloved disciples sleeping.

Once more we went to the Alm Bruderhof. I traveled first and Eberhard came later, staying from the middle of September until the beginning of October when we both returned.

In the last days of September Eberhard had tried to unite the members of the community in the Meal of Remembrance. Our trips back and forth were not without danger, and we had to reckon on the possibility of being dragged off to a concentration camp, like so many, and never reaching our destination.

On our return we found the same sleepy, emotional spirit. Then a severe struggle began. Some of Eberhard's talks from these October and early November days were taken down and later mimeographed and are to be found on the different Bruderhöfe. In the end it became clear to all of us that if we went on like this we were not truly a brotherhood. The brotherhood was dissolved by the agreement of all. There were to be inner meetings, but they would be held in silence. Each one was to go into himself and seek the Spirit of awakening, the uniting Spirit. It was an hour of bitter earnest when we came to this decision. We spoke about a short time. But—what all could happen in a short time!

We had asked for help from the Alm Bruderhof, and those whom they sent—Georg and Moni, Fritz and Sekunda—arrived just before Eberhard had to go in response to a telegram from Professor Zander in Darmstadt. He was to go to Darmstadt for an examination of his bad leg. On November 12 we had a welcome meal for those who had arrived. Before this, however, Eberhard had to leave the Hof. Fritz and I accompanied him as he limped along, as far as the edge of the woods. Who would have thought that this was to be Eberhard's farewell forever?

Difficult days now followed. Already the next day Eberhard received a call to tell him that Professor Zander, our old friend whom we knew from the time of our engagement in 1907, felt an operation was unavoidable. The leg was not healed at all, and might collapse on the street at any moment. He suggested a deeper-going operation which would help the leg to heal, though it would make it shorter. The operation was to take place on Saturday, November 16.

The day before the operation I traveled there to stand by Eberhard. He lay in the hospital in a third-class ward with about three other patients. There he was in bed, in a striped hospital gown, very busy writing a letter to Hans. I asked him whether he would not like to have a room to himself after having such a strenuous time; his mother had expressly asked for this and had sent the money for this purpose. He replied that he wanted to be with and among people!

I was invited to Paul Zander's house for supper. He explained the operation to me, but asked me not to go to Eberhard before the operation, next morning. Before noon, when I arrived at the hospital, the operation was not yet over. Before I went to Eberhard, Dr. Zander told me that it had been a more complicated matter than he had foreseen. The whole operation had been done with only local anaesthesia. So Eberhard had been aware of all that was being done. "They sawed, and hacked, and sewed it up," he said to me.

The week that followed was a hard fight. He did not speak a great deal, at least not in comparison to what our Else said to us during her last weeks. He did not think of pain a great deal. What was very much on his heart was the witness—the witness of Jesus Christ, His life, His words, His death and resurrection, and the pouring out of His Spirit in Jerusalem, with all its consequences. Eberhard often expressed his love for Christ, the dear Christ. He said to me, "When you get home, ask each one: Why do you love Christ?"

At times he lived in the other, the greater world. One of the people who shared the room with him told me after his death, "He was always concerned with God, with the star world and the sun; he was delirious about it at night." There was a young parson who had to visit sick people in the hospital and who had told Eberhard that he wanted to "study" people on these visits. Eberhard told this young man what he thought of this in no uncertain terms! When I told him he should not speak so excitedly, he said, "But I must give witness until the last moment!"

In the last days, when his thoughts often became confused, he once said to me, "Give the girl there, the confirmation candidate, a good book to read." When I said that there was no one there, he said he had just seen someone sitting there in a white dress!

On the Day of Repentance, two days before his death, he asked me in quite a loud voice, "Have you read whether Hitler and Goebbels have repented?" I answered that I hadn't read anything about that in the paper, but that he shouldn't say it so loudly with other people present. This excited him even more, so that he called out very loudly into the room the same question, whether Hitler and Goebbels had repented! (This could have resulted in being put immediately into a concentration camp.)

The evening before the leg was to be amputated, Eberhard had not yet been told that it would have to be done. He asked me that evening to read something about the coming Advent to him. I read the first chapter of the Gospel of John. "And the Word was made flesh, and came to dwell among us; and we saw his glory." He wanted to be alone in the night. He still spoke much about our Rhön Bruderhof and said, "I will think of it in all eternity! And you must go back home and help there." He would have liked to see Hans and Emi-Ma again, especially to help and advise Hans about the Rhön Bruderhof.

The next morning I went very early to see him, together with Moni, who was with me those last days. He was still sleeping when we came. A little later, however, he endorsed a large check for $800 which had come from Johannes Kleinsasser of Millford, Alberta. Shortly before 10 o'clock Paul Zander came in to inform him that he would have to amputate the leg. Eberhard was quite serene and only said, "The surgeon must know, and may God's will be done."

The news which came from the operating room through Moni, who was allowed to be present, did not sound good. The operation took longer than the doctors had anticipated. Meantime Hans and Emi-Ma had arrived from the Alm Bruderhof. After talking on the telephone and being asked to come, they had taken a car the same evening so as to get there as quickly as possible. It was so foggy that they could hardly get through. When they came, they found their father still living; but he did not regain consciousness. Yet we felt very strongly that when we sang to him such songs as "Thee will I love, my strength, my tower," "Jesus is victorious King," and "Yield now, sin and evil deed," he was somehow with us, and we saw how the tears ran down his face. However, he did not speak any more. At 4 o'clock in the afternoon of November 22, 1935, he passed away peacefully. His task, his mission for this period of time, was finished. Incomprehensible! We had not expected it to happen this way, even though during all the last two years we had realized that the time would come when he would no longer be among us.

After the burial we held a special meal in memory of Eberhard. Immediately after this, on November 25, Emi-Ma, Monika and I traveled to the Alm Bruderhof by way of Frankfurt, where we stayed overnight. Almost all the young people were there, including our three sons, Hardi, Heini and Hans Hermann, who were not supposed to come over to Germany because they would have been immediately drafted into the army.

Not long before Eberhard's death, when speaking to a group of guests, he spoke of his own early life and seeking. Just at this point it is fitting to quote what he said then.

> I should like to tell something quite personal. A group of young people often gathered around me, and I tried by means of Bible study and talks to lead people to Jesus. But then there came a time when this was no longer enough. It was a very difficult situation in which I found myself, and I was deeply unhappy. I recognized more and more that this personal dedication to men's souls did not exhaust what Jesus really asked—what is truly God's will. From this time I recognized more and more the need of men, the need of their bodies and souls, their material and social need, their humiliation, their exploitation and their enslavement. I recognized the tremendous power of Mammon, of discord, of hate, and of the sword; I saw the hard boot of the oppressor upon the neck of the oppressed. If a person has not felt and lived these things, he might think such words exaggerated—but they are facts.
>
> Then, in the years from 1913 to 1917, I sought painfully for a deep understanding of the truth. It was clear to me that this purely personal approach does not truly express and fulfill the being of God. I felt that in applying this purely personal approach, this personal Christianity, by concerning myself with other individuals so that they, like myself, might come to this personal Christianity, I was not fulfilling God's will. During these four years I went through a hard struggle. I searched not only in the

old writings, in Jesus' Sermon on the Mount and other Scriptures, but I also sought to know especially the situation of the working classes, the oppressed humanity of the present social order, both from observation and from books, and to share in their life. I did this in order to find a way that would correspond to the way of Jesus, of Francis of Assisi, and also the way of the prophets.

Shortly before the outbreak of the war I wrote to a friend saying that I could not go on like this. I had interested myself in individuals, preached the Gospel, and had endeavored in this way to follow Jesus. I felt that I had to find a way to come to an actual service to mankind; to a dedication which not only was a meeting of individual souls, but a dedication which would establish a monument in real life by which men could recognize the cause for which Jesus died.

The war continued and we saw ever greater horrors; we saw the condition of the men who came home. One young officer came back with both his legs shot off. He came back to his fiancée, hoping to receive the loving care he needed so badly from her, and she informed him that she had become engaged to a man who had a healthy body.

Then the time of hunger came to Berlin. People ate turnips morning, noon and evening. And when the people turned to the officials for money or food in their need and hunger, they were told, "If you are hungry, eat turnips!" On the other hand, even in the middle of Berlin it was still possible for well-to-do "Christian" families to keep a cow and have milk when no one else had milk. And the carts went through the streets bearing the bodies of children who had died, wrapped in newspaper, for there was neither time nor money for a coffin. In 1917 I saw a horse fall in the street; the driver was knocked aside by the starving people who rushed in to cut pieces of meat from the warm body, so that they would have something to bring home to their children and wives.

It was during this time that I visited a poor woman in a basement dwelling. The water was running down the walls of this cellar where she lived. Although she was tubercular, her relatives were living in the same room with her. One could hardly open the window, for the dirt from the feet of the passers-by fell into the room. I offered to find another dwelling for her, but you should have heard what she said. "I'm not going to make a fool of myself; I'll die here where I have lived." And she was a living corpse. After experiences such as these, and also those of the revolutionary times when working people were offered huge rooms and halls with parquet floors, I realized that the whole situation was unbearable. In a talk with a leader of the Student Christian Movement, he told me that a high state official had agreed to work together with me, provided that I remained silent on the great social questions: the war and the terrible suffering.

In our little meetings at our "open house" in Berlin, it became gradually clearer that Jesus' way was a practical one; that He has shown us a real way of life which is more than a way of concern for the soul. It is a way which says very simply, "If you have two coats, give one to him who has none; give food to the hungry, and do not turn away your neighbor when he needs to borrow from you. And when you are asked for an hour's work, give two. But you must strive for His justice. If you want to found a family, then see that all others who want to found a

family are able to do so. If you wish education, work, and
satisfying activity, make these possible for other people
also. If you say that it is your duty to care for your own
health, then accept this duty for the health of others also.
Treat men in the same way that you would be treated by
them. In this is the Law and the Prophets. Enter through
this narrow gate, for this is the way that leads to the
Kingdom of God."

When this became clear to us, we saw that one can go
this way only when one becomes as poor as a beggar and
takes upon oneself, as Jesus did, the whole religious and
moral need of men. Then we become bearers of suffering,
and we suffer because we see how injustice is conquering
the world. We can be of undivided heart only when we
hunger for justice more than for water and bread. Then
we will be persecuted for the sake of this justice. It is only
then that our righteousness will be greater than that of
the moralists and theologians; we will then be filled with
a new fire and a new spirit and warmth from out of the
vital energy of God because we have received the Holy
Spirit.

In this connection it became clear to me that the first
Christian community in Jerusalem was more than a
historical happening; rather, it was here that the Sermon
on the Mount came to life.

It is necessary today as it never has been that we renounce the last vestige of our privilege and rights and let
ourselves be won for this way of total love; the love that
will pour itself out over the land from the breath of the
Holy Spirit; the love that was born out of the first Church-
community.

And so we came to feel that we could not endure the

life that we were living any longer. Although I admit
that I have sacrificed my personal health and that of my
children, I must bear witness to the fact that Jesus concerned Himself not only with souls, but also with bodies.
He made the blind see, the lame walk, and the deaf hear.
He served men's bodies and souls. And He prophesied
and foretold a Kingdom, a rule of God which was to
change completely the conditions and the order of the
world and make them new. To acknowledge this, to
live according to this  this I believe is God's command
for this hour.

# THE FIGHT GOES ON

THE DAYS AND WEEKS that followed Eberhard's death are difficult to write about and difficult to remember. Above all, the brotherhood needed to be restored and newly founded. We all were greatly shaken—especially those at the Rhön Bruderhof, but also at the Alm Bruderhof.

How many guests had told us that very summer that a life like ours would last only as long as Eberhard and our enthusiastic and convinced beginning members were still living. After their death, people said, the whole thing would crumble. In answer to this Eberhard had always said that it would be that way with *human* establishment, but that true community could be founded and supported by the Holy Spirit alone.

This would have to be proven here again. For, as I tried to tell in the beginning, it was not by any human personality or attempt to imitate that this community had been called into life. It had come into being out of the atmosphere of the time after the First World War, when people had come to the end of all they knew, of all their previous means of living and their ideals. From all sides the question came, "What shall we do?" It was this way again after Eberhard's death, so unexpected for us at that moment.

Certain ones, including Hans and Georg, also Fritz and others, stayed behind at the Rhön Bruderhof. A hard fight against a number of weaknesses was going on among us, especially against emotionalism, which is always a disturbance in a community, but also against sin and unfaithfulness, gossip, cliquish friendship and groups, self-pity and excessive sympathy for others. It is hard to understand these things in a time when true heroism against the Hitler spirit and false religion was so sorely needed. And it was in this hour that Eberhard, our oldest friend, counselor and spiritual guide, left us!

Thus we were all called to action. For me and my children who were specially hard-hit because they still needed their father so much, this was a help in getting over the pain of parting from him and missing him. And who was not especially affected? I am thinking of all the young children who were taken in and brought up in our family, but also of the many young people who had lost their fatherly friend and adviser.

Now the call was Unity! All hands on deck! Each individual had to clarify his position and take an attitude to Eberhard's question, "Why do you love Christ?" But there were some who did not find their way so quickly. And perhaps we, especially I, could have found a better, more conciliatory way. At that time I did not recognize so strongly as later that all the same weaknesses, needs, wrongs and sins had to be fought against over and over again in my heart too—the same things that had to be recognized then by many others.

In spite of having to recognize our weaknesses and wrongs and in spite of the great loss of Eberhard's death, we felt a strong urge to go on building up. In Germany, at the Rhön Bruderhof, our situation was getting more difficult all the time. Difficulties also came up at the Alm Bruderhof even though the neighbors were friendly and well-disposed toward us. We got news that the little country of Liechtenstein would not be in a position to keep young men of military age there if bigger states such as Germany claimed them for military service. Besides this, German passports expired and had to be renewed. So it was with certain ones, including Hardi and Heini.

After the wedding of Heini and Annemarie, these two went to the German consulate in Zurich to get their passports extended, which they were able to do for two months. They were then able to travel immediately to England, where a place—the Cotswold Bruderhof—had been found. About this event, too, one could tell astonishing things, how we were helped again and again.

When Hardi went to the consulate for his passport and papers, he was required to say, "Heil Hitler." When he refused to do this, the papers, which had already been handed to him, were taken from him. Our English sister Edna Percival (now Jory) attempted to get them for him but did not succeed. She was told that the owner of the papers would have to fetch them himself. If he had done this, however, and refused to give the Hitler salute, it could have resulted in his being handed over to Germany.

Our outposts in England, Winifred, Hans, Arnold and Gladys, called on the English government authorities, who were willing to admit Hardi, Edith and baby Eberhard Klaus into the country without papers. They had to take a particular airplane to Croydon, near London, where they were expected at the airport. I accompanied them to the airport at Zurich, and we were very anxious about how things would go. Everything went very well!

It was a different story with our Werner. He had gone on a trip in Switzerland with Kurt to sell our turnery and books,

and they had begun selling our products before receiving a
permit from the police. They had done this because the Alm
Bruderhof was counting so much on the income, even though
it was often only a small amount. They were found out and
put under arrest for several days. Then a note was made on
their passports, saying that they had been expelled from Switzerland. Now as Werner's age group was among the first to be
called up, he could not stay in Liechtenstein. So we tried to
send him to England by plane as soon as possible.

With great pains the money, about 200 francs, was gotten
together; we took him to the Zurich airport in time to catch
the plane, and said farewell to him. Next day we were informed in a telephone call that Werner had been forced to return
to Zurich. The telephone call came late in the evening. We
didn't know whether to cry or laugh! Now we had to think
what to do next. He could not travel through Switzerland,
Austria or France, and certainly not through Germany. The
fact that he had been sent back from London was partly because of his inadequate English and partly because a telephone call made to the address of our people there did not
get through. Now we had to figure out how and by what
route we could get him and the others of his age group safely
to England.

All this was far from easy at that time, for even outside of
Germany we were being closely watched by German agents.
It often happened that persons were pushed or forced over
the border and put into a concentration camp, and were never
heard of again. One day when I was in Zurich to do some
shopping, I went into a restaurant and picked up a newspaper.
There I found a short paragraph about Werner headed, "A
remarkable apostle from Zurich forced to go back there."

Our deliberations about how to get the group of young

Germans to England resulted in the formation of a group of strolling players with lutes, guitars and flutes, under the leadership of Hans Meier. They were to get over to England either by sea from Genoa or overland. Again, this came in an amazing way. They chose to go by land, intending to travel through France by night after crossing the Alps. At the customs station there a very sleepy young man appeared, who only looked at Hans' Swiss passport and simply let the others go through! In the train toward the coast on the way to England they were also lucky. Although they were asked why their passports contained no mention of their entry into France, they were allowed to travel on. It was like a miracle that they got through when there was such strict control everywhere.

During all this time of need and frequent anxiety, the place in England had been found, and in quite a remarkable way. Our friends in England had helped us in many ways, especially with the greenhouse and other things in Liechtenstein. They now offered to take in individually our men who were liable for military service, in places where they could live and work. However, they did not want to give help for a group to come over as a community. But we, and they too, wanted to live in community and build community. This building up of the new life had been the sense in which we had decided that those liable to the draft should leave Germany. It was not to save individuals from the great destruction.

Thus there remained no other course for us than to go looking for opportunities ourselves. A car was rented and the persons mentioned above went driving through different regions of England, looking for a suitable farm to rent or to buy. They had no money, nor had permission been granted by the government for us as foreigners to stay in England!

Full of courage and faith that God would show them the

right way, they set out. After inspecting a number of places, they then found near Ashton Keynes, Wiltshire, the place which was later called the Cotswold Bruderhof. The owner was ready to lease it to us, but he required quite a large part of the payment immediately. Meanwhile the number of those of us arriving from Germany and Liechtenstein had grown, so that there seemed no way out other than to occupy a cottage—the gray cottage, as it was called—before so much as a penny had been paid! And wasn't the owner of the farm astonished on finding people there! He said, "This is not usually done in England." (Nor in other countries, I think.)

Meanwhile brothers were traveling around in different districts in order to get the money together. They went to friends, to anyone who might be interested. Heini, for example, who had come to England at the end of March with his Annemarie on their "honeymoon," even approached companies unfamiliar with us, telling them of our situation and of the persecution by Hitler. A good furniture company in Bristol, Crofton Gane, gave him two hundred pounds (as far as I remember) on his word alone, with little proof. This friend helped us several times later, especially with beds, simple but very good, which we later took to Paraguay and which were still doing good service twenty years afterwards. The others who traveled in this way also received generous help, with the result that at the appointed time we had the money!

Full of joy and thanks we could now go to work on the new place. We wanted our new address to be unknown for as long as possible so that we could build up undisturbed. To our amazement, however, we heard that the next time Hans visited Kassel, an official showed him on the map where our Bruderhof lay!

The struggle continued, especially at the Rhön Bruderhof.

Each day it was like a miracle how we were led through it
all, though during the spring and summer of 1936 we lived
on next to nothing. Hans and I went to the big conference
of Mennonites in Holland, where Eberhard had intended to
go with me. There we gathered many experiences and new contacts. It was there that we for the first time met our friend
Orie Miller, who later was very helpful to us. For example,
when we had to leave England during the Second World
War, he helped us with the resettlement of the whole community in Paraguay.

At this Mennonite conference in Amsterdam in 1936 we
were especially surprised to find how strongly the German
Mennonites of that time had become infected with the spirit of
the times, the spirit of Hitler. There was only *one* bus full of
serious conscientious objectors who went to Vredesheim to
discuss their special situation and responsibility and also to
promise mutual help for those who came into difficulties
through their radical witness. Most of those on this bus were
Americans; there were only a few Europeans, and Hans and
I were the only Germans present. All of us who were there
promised to stand up for true peace and disarmament always
and in every event.

All this of course endangered our return to Germany, since
everything one did was observed and spied upon. Hans went
directly to Germany, while I traveled to England to get to
know the new Bruderhof.

After all the poverty at the Rhön Bruderhof and the Alm
Bruderhof, where even the greatest necessities were hard to
come by, the life in England seemed to me quite well-off. But
here too, like everywhere else, there was often a struggle to
be fought out for the new place. There was a large number of
our young people there, and also some of the older members,
such as our Ria, who so faithfully cared for everybody.

In the fall I was called by telephone to the Alm Bruderhof on account of Monika's back trouble, which we then experienced for the first time. During the winter of 1936–1937 I went to many doctors in Zurich with her, but none of them was able to discover the cause of her trouble.

Shortly before Christmas I went once more—for the last time—to the Rhön Bruderhof. The atmosphere around us there was very thick, and we had a strong feeling already then that some action against us was afoot. When Hans advised me early in April to go once again to Germany if there was anything at the Rhön Bruderhof that I still wanted to arrange or take care of, it was unfortunately already too late.

On April 14, 1937, we were informed by telephone that all residents of the Rhön Bruderhof had to leave the place within twenty-four hours. (The time was then extended another twenty-four hours because of a flu epidemic among the children.) "Not desired in Germany" was the reason for this order. For all of us, both in Germany and outside, this was a great shock, even though all these years we had counted on measures of this kind being taken.

It was surely a good thing that two Hutterian brothers, David Hofer *Vetter* of James Valley, Manitoba, and Michael Waldner *Vetter* of Bon Homme, South Dakota, just happened to be there, having arrived shortly before from England. They now witnessed the whole departure and told about all they experienced in a report and in letters. I would like to end my account of our beginning times with their report on the closing of the Rhön Bruderhof.[1]

April 14th: Michael Waldner and I were in Eberhard Arnold's room writing letters, about 10 a.m. Then Hans Meier opened the door and said, "Brothers, prepare your-

[1] "The Dissolution of the Rhoenbruderhof, From the Diary of the Hutterian Elder, David Hofer." *The Plough*, September 1938, pp. 89–94.

selves, for I have just come from the hill and saw behind the wood a large number of police. They may come to the Bruderhof, but they cannot do anything to you." Then he closed the door and went to his office to tidy up. And as I, thereupon, went to the window and looked out, I saw the police already hurrying down the hill. I went to the door and down to the second storey of the house and out of the corridor to see what would happen.

There were already twenty-five policemen standing at the door. "Where is Hans Meier?" one shouted at once at me. I answered quite simply, "Doubtless in the house." "Call him out here!" was the next order. As I went to Hans Meier's room he met me and introduced himself quite calmly and fearlessly to the police. Then the chief officer read Hans Meier the order. "I inform you herewith that the Rhön-bruderhof is now dissolved by the state and must exist no longer. From now on it is to be called 'Sparhof' and as you are leader of this Bruderhof, I demand all books and keys from you. I inform you also that within twenty-four hours all must leave the place!" * Then he went straight to the office with Hans Meier. The other police surrounded the whole Bruderhof and drove all brothers and sisters, young and old, into the dining room. There they were guarded by two policemen, and no one was allowed either out or in. In the meantime the others searched every room and took whatever they wanted away in their cars. At last they came to our room, where we were still. They ordered us to go to the brothers in the dining room. We went down quite calmly

* The Bruderhof was dissolved on the strength of the law against communistic disturbances (passed 1933), and it was said that "a pacifist and international community was not wanted in Germany." The accusation that the Bruderhof was dissolved for economic reasons is only a pretext, as is proved by the fact that the three executive members had to be set free.

to the brothers and sisters, and found them perplexed and discouraged. Then we encouraged them and told them not to despair.

Then two officials came to us. One carried a typewriter, the other a bundle of papers. They sat down and called each by name, and each had to answer what he was asked, and then the filled-in paper was signed. The paper, however, was only a proclamation regarding registration for mustering—which paper we ourselves examined carefully before it was signed. In the meantime, we saw through the window how all the rooms were searched, and how they carried all that they wanted to their cars. And as I saw that it was nearly time for our room to be searched, I wanted to go out to go to it. But at the door I was held up and told to return to the room. I told them, "I want to go to my room. We are foreigners and do not want our things searched and carried off." He said he was not allowed to let anyone out. "If you want to go out, you must first get permission from our chief officer and bring it to me." I asked, "Where is he?" He said, "Up in the office." I went back and applied to the chief officer, who was occupied with Hans Meier, for the liberty to go to my room, which he granted me.

Then I called Michael Waldner and we went together to our room. Before long, searchers came to our room and began to search. We pointed out to them that we were aliens, and yet German aliens [of German extraction], and did not want to have our things searched. They asked us what we wanted with these people here, where we came from, and what had brought us to these people. We told them, "These people are our brothers in the faith, to whom we have sent much help from America to build up this Bruderhof and are therefore very much interested in what happens here and how things will be with them." We saw at once that our presence was no pleasure to them, and that we were in their way. We asked them to leave us here for a few days. They refused and said that that was no concern of theirs. By now all the brothers and sisters had signed the papers. It was already 3 p.m. when they had finished, and only then were they allowed to have some food. Our food, however, had already been brought to us and we had already eaten.

The police, however, stood outside the dining room and spoke together. Then I went out to them and began to speak to them about this occurrence. I told them that what we had experienced here today was quite uncalled for, and that we had not expected such a thing of Germany. I thought they would have treated their citizens and peasants better than we had been forced to see and experience that day. I told them that they were worse than the Americans. Then they at once asked me, "How?" I told them that we as Germans were called up in the last war to do military service against Germany. We objected and refused to do it, as these, our brothers, had just done. Then we asked our government in U.S.A. to let us have the freedom to leave the country, as we could not obey it in doing military service. We asked to sell all we had and to leave nothing behind us—all of which was not refused us by the government; but during wartime we were allowed to emigrate to Canada, and this under government protection that nothing might happen to us. I asked them why they could not treat this community so. Then they said to me, "Why can't you show your obedience to the government like the others, and do as it says?" I told them clearly that we respected the government highly, but that we could not obey what it demanded against our conscience. Then he asked me, "To what extent?" I told them that the Word of God says I must love my neighbor and not kill him, and for this reason we could not follow and obey the government. Then another spoke and said, "Friend, have you not read that our Saviour said, 'I have not come to send peace but the sword,' and that he also told his disciples to buy swords? Why do you not believe these passages of the scriptures?" I told him how I understood these passages. Then he said my interpretation was wrong. He said, "If the whole world consisted of angels, like all of you, then there would be no need of war, but you know that men are not all so." "And we also do not want war," they insisted. "We only want to make ourselves strong, because all fear the strong. If we are weak then all walk over us, but if we are strong, they fear us, and for this reason we prepare for war, not because we want to fight."

The others thought the brothers and sisters were taking too long to eat and asked, "Have they a whole ox to wolf up in there that they are taking so long about it?" After the meal they ordered the whole community to assemble outside the door. Michael Waldner and I were also ordered, as though they had a proclamation to read out. I soon saw, however, that they only wanted to take photographs, and left the line saying to Michael Waldner, "Come into the house." To them I said, "We do not need that." Then the order was read that the Bruderhof was now dissolved, and that now no Bruderhof existed in Germany. None of them was to dare to take anything connected with the farm or the property of the community, or household goods, etc., with him, for it would only result in much searching if one of them dared to take any of the household goods, with which order they all left the place.

We, however, the whole community, met for prayer with very troubled and sorrowful hearts. We told God of our need and distress and earnestly prayed him not to leave us in this difficult time and situation, but to give us true understanding and wisdom to act according to his will and counsel, as his children. Yes, to be our counsellor himself, and to remain our leader and not forsake us.

After the prayer we considered how things stood, and how we could bring it about that the community might remain together. For the godless men wanted to scatter all the brothers and sisters over Germany, by sending them to their relatives. Also we wanted badly to let the community in England and the one in Liechtenstein know what was happening here at the Rhönbruderhof.

So it was first seen that Arno Martin, the steward of the Almbruderhof in Liechtenstein, who was just about to go there, should be sent to Liechtenstein to tell Hans Zumpe and also the community in England this news, as soon as he was over the German frontier. But how were we to send anyone as the police had robbed us of all our money—over 400 marks? Thus there was not a cent in the hands of the community, because it had been robbed of everything, including keys and books, and all common rooms were closed and locked. So it was necessary to give the brothers and sisters our travelling money, and we, Hans Meier and I, went with Arno Martin to Schlüchtern, arriving there at twelve midnight, and there we saw him off with the sad news which he was to send to the Cotswold Bruderhof and to Liechtenstein.

Hans Meier and I returned with heavy hearts to the community, and found all still up. We then went to rest but slept little.

April 15th: Arose once more in health, for which much thanks to God. Had also some breakfast. We were in our rooms for half an hour after eating, when Hans Meier came in, in very great haste, and told us that a gentleman from Fulda was in the yard with his car, demanding that the executive committee go with him to Fulda to settle some trifling matters, that they might then be able to leave. This news was an unhappy surprise for me. I did not believe the word of the gentleman from Fulda at all. I said to Michael Waldner, "Do you believe that these brothers will be back by midday, as he promises?" Michael Waldner said, "I don't know, still he promises it." I said, "We shall see when the time comes." Hans Meier, Hans Boller and Karl Keiderling got ready in great haste and left.

The whole community waited with longing at twelve o'clock, but no brothers came. Two o'clock came, and four o'clock—the brothers did not come. Then Michael Waldner and I went to the wood on the hill where they should arrive. Then we saw a car come, and recognized it at once as the car that took the brothers away. We went to it. A man got out and came to us. I asked, "Where are the brothers?" "They have not come," was the answer.* Immediately afterwards he ordered me to call the whole community together. "We have a letter to read to you from the brothers." First he read us the command to leave the place within twenty-four hours. Then that the government was willing to let us take our five brothers of military age with us, and that at the request of the three brothers in Fulda, the whole community was to be permitted to leave together. The brothers and sisters were glad that they had given up their previous intention of scattering them to their relatives all over Germany. So they all signed a letter that they would

* These three brothers were imprisoned for three months on a charge of fraud, which was later withdrawn and they were set free.

leave the Bruderhof and go to the other communities. As however several brothers and sisters had no passports, and as we wanted to see the brothers in prison regarding their families, before leaving, I asked the chief officer for a written note permitting me to see the brothers in Fulda, which he gave me. When everything was settled, they departed.

We, however, gathered together for prayer, and comforted ourselves by the word of God. I read Psalm 3 as an admonition to us, thanked God from the heart that he had so changed and directed matters that the community could go to the other communities, prayed ardently to God not to forsake us in this great trouble and sorrow, and to send his guardian angel to watch over and protect us.

After the prayer, preparations were made for the journey. We advised them to get today as much food as they could from the pantry, as provision for the journey. For it was *their* store of food, so that they should take what they needed.

Next morning at five o'clock, our six brothers and sisters left for Neuhof to go to the law office in Fulda regarding passports. I also went with them to see the brothers in prison, and brought them the news that today at 6 p.m. the whole community would leave Germany, with their wives and families. The brothers rejoiced greatly that the community was caring so faithfully for their wives and children.

I encouraged the imprisoned brothers as well as I could to be patient—the loving gracious God would not forsake them. It was very hard for all the brothers and sisters to leave the results of the sweat of their brows and depart empty-handed. I took leave of the brothers with a heavy heart and went again to the law office to the other brothers and sisters, to get the passports as quickly as possible and to arrange about the tickets—all of which meant much work for the officials. When all was finished, we returned home. We arrived safely at the Bruderhof at 4 p.m. and found Michael Waldner and all the brothers and sisters busy packing and preparing for the journey. At 5 p.m. we had a little to eat, after which we met again for prayer—for the last time at the Rhönbruderhof. We prayed fervently to God to keep, watch and protect his Church on this journey which we were about to begin, trusting in his faithful promise not to forsake us, but through his protection and grace to accompany us and bring us in peace to his children in the other communities. All of which our dear God faithfully performed. He has faithfully helped us all, so that we have come in health to the Church again.

As it had rained all day, and especially in the afternoon, we were anxious about the sick children and a sick sister, for we had over a mile to go over the hills to the lorries or trucks and they might catch cold on the way. When the hour arrived, however, and all stood ready to leave, suddenly the sun shone brightly. The rain had ceased and the sun shone down on us. That was to us a wonder and grace of God and we thanked him in our hearts for this loving act.

Now the brothers and sisters began to climb the hill with their sick children and the sick sister, with the little bundles which each had to carry on his back. Michael Waldner carried a child on his back. I carried a large bundle for Hans Meier's wife, who had a few days previously given birth to a child. We were all laden, all had hands and backs full. Thus with heavy hearts and perturbed feelings we climbed the hill. We stopped several times and looked at the beautifully built Bruderhof, the loved home which we had had to leave so suddenly and unexpectedly. Some went to the burial ground to the grave of our beloved Eberhard Arnold and saw it for the last time.

When we arrived at the place, the cars were already there. Then everything was put in and when they were loaded and everyone had got in, they set off to the station. Michael Waldner, Hella Römer[2] and I were the only ones left at the Rhönbruderhof. With sad and deeply perturbed hearts we found the place empty. We went early to rest, but uneasiness did not let us get much sleep. Next morning we began to tidy the rooms. But the picture that met us cannot be described. Uneaten food stood on the tables. The bedclothes lay in confusion on the beds. In the kindergarten the playthings and furniture lay as the children had left them. In the laundry the clothes lay unwashed, soaking partly in tubs and partly in the boiler. It was a perfect wilderness, enough to make the heart break and the eyes weep.

Such a thing we had till then neither experienced nor seen. The wilderness was horrible. It seemed as though we had had to come to Europe to experience and learn what it means to be driven from one's house and home. God has protected us in America up till now from such misery, for which we owe him thanks. Although during the war we had to emigrate to Canada, that emigration was not to be compared with this ejection.

This is a short account of how the Rhönbruderhof in Germany came to an end and was dissolved by the German government.

*David Hofer*

[2] Our bookkeeper, who had to close the books and present them to the authorities. (We were charged with "fraudulent bankruptcy"!) She was released several weeks later.

# POSTSCRIPT TO THE SECOND EDITION

THE CLOSING of the Rhön Bruderhof in 1937 did not bring about the intended extinction of the tiny movement but made it spread slowly to other people and to other countries. We were given asylum in England, where all were finally gathered safely together again for several years. War with Germany, however, gave no other choice to the always fair and friendly Home Office than to intern our alien members or to permit us to emigrate.

With the advice and help of our Mennonite friend, Orie Miller, we emigrated to Paraguay, South America, the only country offering a home during the war years. Despite the unbelievable obstacles to settling in such large numbers in a semi-tropical wilderness, we were grateful to be allowed to live together in community. By 1961, after more than twenty years in South America, we were able to move once again to the northern hemisphere, where we were attracted to the United States by the greater interest in our life.

On the 21st of June, 1970, at our New York community, we celebrated the fiftieth anniversary of the beginning of our community life in Sannerz, Germany. All the members from our three communities met in thankfulness for the recent years of closer contact in one country, for the return to publishing under the name "Plough Publishing House," for the livelihood given us from "Community Playthings" (educational play equipment), and above all for the gift of unity coming again and again during these fifty years in spite of all our failings and weaknesses.

For the present we are looking toward the founding of a fourth place, hopefully in Europe again, as our three communities in the United States are reaching optimum size. All of us who joined the Bruderhof movement since the closing of the Rhön Bruderhof find here the possibility to give ourselves with others in the everyday struggle and joy of living in brotherhood. It is no utopian escape. We face a fragment of world need in ourselves and in our neighbors and strive for an answer to it. (If we are honest, which human can face more than a fragment?) It is an illusion to think that men, women, and children can live together in this world today in such a way as to escape its need and sickness, for the "world" situation is everywhere "our" situation whether we live in full community or try to drop out of society, whether we move to suburbia or stay in the "normal" urban or rural mainstream.

We are very well aware of the fact of human weakness and our own weakness. We are aware of the fact that as individuals or as communities we are capable of losing the way. But we believe that discipleship of Jesus is a clear way of love, of freedom, and of truth in deeds, and that we can be given the strength again and again to strive for it and to follow it freely and wholeheartedly. We seek fresh courage, hope, and faith to live in truer unity and brotherhood, wishing for the same living spirit of the early Christians and of the early years of Emmy Arnold's story to touch us constantly afresh—to touch our lives, the life of our communities, and the life of all men.

With Eberhard Arnold we affirm: "This planet, the Earth, must be conquered for a new Kingdom, for a new order, for a new unity, for a new joy. This joy must come to us from the God who is the God of love, who is the Spirit of peace and of unity and community. That is the message Jesus brings. And Jesus had the faith and the certainty that this message can be believed today."

*Douglas A. Moody*
June 1971